CW01626551

WHAT YING ABOUT MELVIN PILLAY

"Melvin, I love your enthusiasm. What a privilege it is for you to be here with us, where you also honored God so wonderfully well and so excitingly."

—Zig Ziglar

"Melvin Pillay is a gifted life coach who knows how to unlock the best out of any individual with love and care."

—Ambassador Samuel Fidelis

"Understanding success is one of the major challenges of today's world. Melvin Pillay shares how to gain true success not only at work but also at home. This teaching results from Melvin's practical living, which came from more than twenty-five years of research on this topic."

—Tamrat Layne, Former Prime Minister of Ethiopia

"Melvin Pillay is a rare find. For all who read these words, I hope that you have at least one chance to encounter Melvin sometime in your life."

—Perry Marshall

How Melvin Turned around My Business in 60 Days!

"**I** met Melvin by reaching out to him on LinkedIn one day, not knowing he was a kingdom believer like me. We met by divine appointment! He is my prophetic mentor, and I'm honored to call him my friend. When I think about challenges I faced, there were numerous times Melvin shared messages of biblical encouragement that somehow aligned with what I was thinking at the time, without me ever telling him what I was going through! My business was going to the pits—nearing $0 in revenue. When Melvin officially became my prophetic mentor, in sixty days my business became a six-figure company! Why? Because he saw more in me than I did in myself. I thank God for sending Melvin my way to help me fulfill my purpose in my life. He is a true prophetic voice of our time!

—Mathew Thomas, Dallas, Texas

The Real Deal

"Melvin is one of the most authentic, kind, generous, and trustworthy individuals you'll ever meet! He masterfully brings the Word of God alive through his teachings, and has brought spiritual clarity to many individuals. But one of Melvin's greatest talents is teaching people how to do business God's way, not man's way.

"(Hint: God's way is much easier than man's way, and it produces much greater results.) So, if you're looking for something more, then your search is over. Reach out to Melvin now; you'll be thankful that you did!"

—Brian Winter, Lake Orion, Missouri

A True Difference-Maker

"Melvin has been a true difference-maker for me . . . in my business and in my life. My whiteboard session with him was a profound experience that literally changed things in me. And over time, he has given me important words that couldn't have been more perfectly timed. If you ever have the opportunity to speak with Melvin, you owe it to yourself—and to those you influence—to do so!"

—Jim Lange, Sylvania, Ohio

UNWORK

God's Design for
Man's Freedom from Hard Work

MELVIN PILLAY

Unwork: God's Design for Man's Freedom from Hard Work/Melvin Pillay

Copyright © 2023 by Royal Pillay Acquisitions, www.melvinpillay.com.

All rights reserved. This book or any portion thereof may not be reproduced or used in any manner whatsoever without the express written permission of the publisher except for the use of brief quotations in a book review. For permission requests, write to Royal Pillay Acquisitions via email:

support@melvinpillay.com.

The author and publisher shall not be liable for your misuse of this material. This book is for strictly informational and educational purposes.

For information about special discounts for bulk purchases, please contact Royal Pillay Acquisitions via email: support@melvinpillay.com.

Unless otherwise indicated, all scripture is taken from the HOLY BIBLE, NEW INTERNATIONAL VERSION®. NIV®. Copyright © 1973, 1978, 1984 by International Bible Society. Used by permission of Zondervan. All rights reserved worldwide.

Scriptures marked AMP are taken from the Amplified® Bible (AMP). Copyright © 2015 by The Lockman Foundation Used by permission. www.Lockman.org.

Scriptures marked CJB are from the Complete Jewish Bible by David H. Stern. Copyright © 1998. All rights reserved. Used by permission of Messianic Jewish Publishers, 6120 Day Long Lane, Clarksville, MD 21029. www.messianicjewish.net.

Scriptures marked ESV are from The Holy Bible, English Standard Version ® (ESV ®), copyright © 2001 by Crossway, a publishing ministry of Good News Publishers. Used by permission. All rights reserved.

All Scripture marked with the designation "GW" is taken from *GOD'S WORD*®. © 1995, 2003, 2013, 2014, 2019, 2020 by God's Word to the Nations Mission Society. Used by permission.

Scriptures marked KJV are taken from the King James Version of the Bible, public domain.

Scripture quotations marked (NASB) are taken from the New American Standard Bible ®, Copyright © 1960, 1962, 1963, 1968, 1971, 1972, 1973, 1975, 1977, 1995 by The Lockman Foundation. Used by permission.

Scripture quotations marked (NLT) are taken from the *Holy Bible, New Living Translation*, copyright © 1996, 2004, 2007, 2013 by Tyndale House Foundation. Used by permission of Tyndale House Publishers, Inc., Carol Stream, Illinois 60188. All rights reserved.

Printed in the United States of America.

ISBN: 978-0-473-70214-4

CONTENTS

To all the hard workers of the past who were taught to reward hard work with more work—welcome to unwork.

FOREWORD

I remember reading *The 4-Hour Workweek* by Timothy Ferris, close to when it first came out, when I was in my early thirties, just as I was embarking on a portfolio life as a follower of Jesus. And since then, I have adopted effective life hacks to juggle and balance competing demands on my time as a leader operating in multiple spheres. By the grace of God, much of this knowledge and the habits that have formed from reading and learning have made a major difference. But something was missing. The changes alleviated the symptoms well but had not identified the cause, nor provided the cure.

Meeting with Melvin, and reading his book *Unwork*, has clarified what that missing factor is, one which even the best, most organized people can overlook: our own hearts and earthly thoughts, or what Melvin calls "humanistic thinking." We have become enslaved by the curse of hard work, infected by the thinking that the success that may or may not come from it is the only way to go. Actually, as Melvin elegantly and super-efficiently articulates, with evident divine help from our Maker above, the only way is to stop, listen, and obey. To *unwork*.

Instead of just relying on earthly gurus, we meet to receive instructions from the Author himself of work and rest. We break free from our enslavement to the mindsets that stop us truly fulfilling our destinies by entering the presence of God and becoming his friends, thereby enjoying his blessings. I cannot say I am there yet, but with the insights from this book and the help of the Holy Spirit, I am already beginning to enjoy greater rest, favor, abundance, and time for the people and activities that matter most in life.

Only when we learn to *unwork* will we truly be able to do our best work and not fill the rest of the time with that which is unnecessary, that which arises from our restlessness, and that which has no eternal value. Can we all, like Melvin, only work one day a week or less and be at rest the other six days? Why not? In God anything is possible. If we truly believe he can still a storm and part a sea, then surely, we must be able to trust him to give us the insights needed to thrive. We can use our time for his glory well, without the need to worry or to be anxious. In him we find all the answers. He is the answer.

Imagine what the world would look like if more people joined the *unwork* movement? Would we have fewer mental health problems in what seems to be a post-COVID pandemic of anxiety? Would we make greater progress on the global issues we face today, whether environmental, economic, or societal? Would entire populations not discover a way out of poverty, both physical and mental? Most certainly.

Melvin's work as a speaker and mentor has already transformed many hundreds if not thousands of lives. As more embrace the wisdom gleaned in *Unwork*, the potential for millions, if not billions, to experience life transformation is there to be unlocked. Coming, myself, from a Protestant background as the son of missionaries, and being from Asia originally, it can be hard to swallow a message that excessive work is neither good nor desired by God, for surely having a hard work ethic must yield results? But the stress, breakdown, and relational damage I have experienced and witnessed around me over the years bears testimony to the curse of work idolatry. The truth is we have ignored and misinterpreted Scripture at great cost to us in our lives, time, and treasure. It is time to heed the Author's words and to see rest no more as a brief respite on a Sabbath or at night, but as a permanent state of being in him to which we are continuously being recalled.

—**Lord Wei** of Shoreditch,

Member of the House of Lords of the United Kingdom with an interest in social impact,

previous advisor to Downing Street,

sits on and has chaired multiple boards in the worlds of business, technology, philanthropy, and ministry

PREFACE

We are born to play.

When we were small, we were encouraged to play. People bought us toys and took us places to have fun, and we loved it and enjoyed it.

Playing is innate; it is a spiritual trait God gifts us all with, and it is no wonder—the benefits of play are numerous. Play improves cognitive, physical, social, and emotional well-being. In other words, playing makes one smarter, healthier, happier, more connected, and more successful.

Listen to what Wisdom says:

> I was with him as someone he could trust. For me, every day was pure delight, as I played in his presence all the time, playing everywhere on his earth and delighting in humankind.
> —Proverbs 8:30–31

Then one day play was taken away from us with these words: Stop playing and act your age. You are not a child anymore. Get a job and work hard and make something of your life.

Suddenly life went from play to work, and our safe world changed from games to battles, from a playground to a war zone. Work became a fight.

Then one day you visited Grandma at the old people's home, and she was busy playing games and having fun because the experts said that there were numerous benefits to play. They said:

Playing makes one smarter, healthier, happier, more connected, and more successful.

You scratch your head and think to yourself, *Did I miss something*? Children are encouraged to play; old people are encouraged to play; but everybody else is told to *work* hard.

No wonder global health organizations say there is a significant increase in mental illness around the world. Stress levels are at an all-time high, and even with all our stuff and amazing technology, we are far less happy. Could the 1659 saying by J. Howell be right? Maybe it's even a prophecy: All work and no play make Jack a dull boy.

In Our Minds, in Our Mouths

The word *work* is common, and frequently used in our daily conversations. For example, we say things like:

This combination seems to *work.*

I will check my calendar to see if that time will *work.*

This partnership does not *work.*

And of course, the big one—I am going to *work!*

From being young adults to becoming old people, our days are filled with work.

We go to work for ourselves.

We go to work for our children.

We go to work for others.

We go to work for God.

But nobody lives by the startling truth that *God goes to work for us*, and he asks us to wait for him.

The word "wait" in Hebrew is *kawa*, which means "entwining," like the way two ropes are intertwined—there is no way to see where one starts or the other ends. The two ropes become one.

The prophet Isaiah proclaimed,

> From days of old no one has heard, nor has ear perceived,
> Nor has the eye seen a God besides You,
> Who works *and* acts in behalf of the one who [gladly] waits for Him.
> —Isaiah 64:4 AMP

It is time for us to play again; it is time for us to understand work. It is time for us to *unwork*. And just maybe we will light a fire of an *unwork reformation*, an *unwork restoration*, and an *unwork revolution* that shall never be put out, for the glory of Jesus Christ.

Melvin Pillay

INTRODUCTION

If hard work made one rich, the African woman would be a billionaire.
—African Proverb

"As he thinks in his heart, so is he [in behavior]" (Proverbs 23:7 AMP) is one of the most quoted of King Solomon's wise sayings. How we think about a certain thing as young children will be how we view it all our life, and also how we live all our days on earth. This is called our state of mind, and it determines everything.

Retraining the Mind

From birth, every traumatic experience and harmful negative thing leads to developing the brain's negative state of mind. Conversely, positive and uplifting things lead to the brain's positive state of mind. Therapists using cognitive behavioral therapy (CBT) can help people change their state of mind by getting them to practice positive emotions and positive emotional viewpoints so that an individual can break the pattern of negative anticipation. This means our state of mind, which is either negative or positive, can be taught to create new anticipation.

Amazingly, our very thoughts often become our reality, thereby acting as self-fulfilling prophecies.

James, the Lord's disciple, was like an early adopter of CBT. He taught us to "consider it pure joy, my brothers and sisters, whenever you face trials of many kinds" (James 1:2) because he knew our state of mind would determine the outcome of our life.

I encourage you to cultivate a positive state of mind rather than a negative one. We will all encounter painful, life-altering moments. When you lose a loved one or something traumatic happens, it can put you in a state of grief or depressed emotions. But the longer you stay in that state, the harder it is for you to break out of it and the more permanent that emotion becomes. A positive state of mind will help you overcome, break through, and break free faster from grief and emotional depression.

The State of Mind of Work

Another state of mind issue is toward work. Children view *work* as being hard and meaningless, a bad thing that takes Mom and Dad away.

> "We needed you, but you ignored us."
>
> "You even left us with strangers at daycares or with other relatives while you went to the place called 'work.'"
>
> "You could not give us your time; work took it all."

We witnessed our parents work hard, long hours, telling us "I am doing it for you." And so, our state of mind about work was formed. We started to believe that hard work is productive and rest is unproductive. The longer this remained as our state of mind, the more permanent it became, and we created the anticipation of a life of hard work as a "good" thing.

But hard work has always been a form of discipline for those who strayed from the Word of God and defied his wisdom.

Moses understood this, and he penned these words:

> Some lived in darkness, in death-dark gloom,
> bound in misery and iron chains,
> because they defied God's word,
> scorned the counsel of the Most High.
> So he humbled their hearts by hard labor;
> when they stumbled, no one came to their aid.
> —Psalm 107:10–12 CJB

Today, figuratively speaking, countless millions are living in death-dark gloom, bound by the misery and iron chains of hard work. Surely it is time for us to be set free and find a better way to live and work.

Crack the Unwork Code

Unwork does not mean we should *not* work, neither does it mean to be lazy or idle or despise work. *Unwork* is about learning how to work smart; it's about cracking the code of a perfect work-life balance.

It means you can:

1. Find the true state of mind about work and work God's way.
2. Understand the timing: Do not go when it's time to wait. Do not wait when it's time to go.
3. Know the seasons: Do not slumber during the harvest season. Do not overwork during the winter season. "For everything there is a season and a right time for every intention under heaven" (Ecclesiastes 3:1).

Be Encouraged!

After more than two decades of research and teaching these kingdom truths to leaders, business owners, and entrepreneurs from around the world, I sensed a leading to write this little book to encourage, strengthen, and help fellow believers accomplish the call of God on their lives. Through the wind and the waves, the trials and the storms, I pray that you are inspired with the knowledge that the goodness and love of God follows you all the days of your life.

You were not made for work.

You were made for God.

1

THE PRINCIPLE OF HARD WORK

First, you think it, then you feel it, then you become it. Hard work or unwork? The choice is yours.

In 1860 or thereabouts, my ancestors were taken from India by the British, put on ships, and shipped to South Africa. They were the modern-day indentured laborers or slaves of their time. Many of them were abused, beaten, and killed. Women were raped, and child labor was rampant. Their masters frequently worked their Indian slaves to death, forcing them to work from sunrise to sunset in the sugarcane fields. Often given little or no food, and tortured if they dared try to escape, many committed suicide; it was easier than living under such a system. This is my heritage, and hard work was the curse passed down through the generations.

A Generational Curse

A generational curse is not a mystical thing or folklore. It is a real thing, and it is evident even in the twenty-first century. For example, in the mid-1960s, Canadian psychiatrist Vivian Rakoff and colleagues documented unusually high rates of psychological distress amongst children of holocaust survivors. Their research led to what is today known as generational trauma.

Just as good genes include good health, intelligence, and good looks, so do bad genes contain traits of disease, poor health, and poverty. So, too, do we inherit from our parents and ancestors blessings and curses. These things affect us in daily life, and if not dealt with, they become our reality and then are passed on to our children and their children. It never ends until somebody recognizes the curse and deals with it spiritually, mentally, emotionally, and physically.

The principle of hard work is a generational curse that was passed down to us from our ancestors.

It has caused us all so much pain and keeps us enslaved in a ruthless, vicious cycle. Jesus freed us from this curse. Let's claim victory and receive wisdom and blessings.

When a Good Principle Goes Bad

A principle can be a beautiful thing; however, many have experienced moments when a good principle goes bad.

I grew up in a little village called Tin Town, and our home was a tin shack built from nailing together pieces of sheet metal and tree branches. I started my first part-time job in 1987, when I was ten years old. It was hard work. I was paid to travel around the rural villages and collect scrap metal with other children. Most of the time we would find old, abandoned cars that we had to chop into small pieces using metal axes. It was hard labor, painful and dangerous, and full of long hours. I narrowly escaped death on numerous occasions—when I accidently stepped on venomous snakes, or disturbed wild animals, or was attacked by local villagers who were angered by my collecting their scrap metal.

The pay was approximately fifty cents a day. It was not a lot but enough to buy a little bit of food for my family. I was very grateful to the man who employed me. Growing up in abject poverty in rural South Africa during the apartheid regime was far from easy, and every little cent helped to keep us fed. I decided that I had to be the hardest-working person in the field if I wanted to be a success, please the boss, and not starve. This principle of hard work being the only way to live was deposited in my mind, etched upon my heart, and felt in my emotions.

Believing this principle to be true was unfortunate and the result of wrong thinking, but I had learned this from people around me. In my tiny community, everybody suffered. Poverty was the only thing we knew, and we believed hard work was the only way to live.

Religion and Principles

I was not born into a Christian family. My life as a child was filled with learning about several different worldviews and religions, and Christianity's principles of leadership, work, and success seemed fundamentally the same as every other religion's that I studied or practiced... until one day these words were impressed upon me:

CHRISTIANITY DOES NOT HAVE JUST GOOD PRINCIPLES;
IT HAS A GOOD, JUST PRINCE.

A principle is a primary truth, and all other truths hang on it. The problem is that principles can be interpreted and applied incorrectly, and this is often the case. Tradition, culture, and even religion can cause the harm they do because of stubborn viewpoints and beliefs that are built on untrue principles. A principle can also be an abstract thing holding no firm meaning whereas the Prince, Jesus Christ, is a real person. He is the way, the truth, and the life. There is no other way to interpret the Prince. So, after much prayer and reflecting, I stopped seeking good principles and started seeking the good Prince.

2

GOD'S PRECEPTS VERSUS HUMAN CONCEPTS

I love old English. For example, a biblical verse in old English reads like this: "Thus saith the Lord, The heaven is my throne, and the earth is my footstool" (Isaiah 66:1 KJV). That's a precept of God. It is a thought of God, and it cannot be changed. It cannot be worded differently or interpreted to suit our subjective reasoning. God meant what he said. And that's it. Another example of a precept is, "Before I formed you in the womb I knew you, before you were born I set you apart; I appointed you as a prophet" (Jeremiah 1:5).

When you receive a prophetic word from God, it is a precept of God. It cannot be changed or challenged. Sadly, most people do not believe this.

- ✓ A precept of God will scare you.
- ✓ A precept of God will overwhelm you.
- ✓ A precept of God will show you how little you have in terms of resources to get a thing done.

Human Concepts

A concept is an abstract idea or general notion our limited human thoughts feed us. How we think about things affects how we think about God and his precepts about us. King David understood this when he said, "Make me understand the way of Your precepts, so that I will meditate (focus my thoughts) on Your wonderful works" (Psalm 119:27 AMP).

Whenever God speaks, he gives his precept. The issue is we receive it through the filters of our limited human concepts. We reason and think about how much money we have in our bank account, how much energy we have, how large a team we've got. These are all concepts that are human concepts.

Humanistic Concepts

I'll go one step further. Very often our concepts are humanistic. This is why Jesus constantly said to the disciples, "You of little faith, why are you so afraid?" He went even further. "You unbelieving and perverse generation," Jesus replied, "how long shall I stay with you? How long shall I put up with you?"

Did Jesus say that?

Absolutely—you can read his words in Matthew 8:26 and 17:17.

Jesus loved his disciples, but he often corrected and rebuked them because of doubt, unbelief, and fear. I believe that God was saying to them, "I am the reality. I am here. I am giving you my precept. Why do you reason with human concepts?"

Think about the amazing encounter Peter and the disciples had. They were in a boat and Jesus came to them, walking on water. Peter called out and Jesus replied, "Come." Peter got out of the boat and walked not on water but on the word of Jesus. Jesus spoke a precept and Peter walked in its reality. However, the winds and waves rose, and Peter took his eyes off the reality of God's precept. He looked to the right and to the left and the human concept came in and the precept went away (Matthew 14:28–30). So, the battle is between precepts and concepts.

God's word is a precept.
Our reasoning is a concept.

Our concepts are so powerful, they stop the precepts of God from unfolding in our midst.

Do Not Worry

Okay, walking on water is not something that we plan on doing daily. Perhaps this precept may be closer to home. The precept "Do not worry" is something we all can relate to.

I often wondered about the antidote for worry. Jesus said "Do not worry about your life" (Matthew 6:25). This is nothing strategic, nothing practical, and offers no application from a human concept. But it is the *only* cure. Do not worry but "seek first his kingdom and his righteousness, and all these things will be given to you" (Matthew 6:33). The cure reminds me of the story about when the children of Israel were bitten by snakes in the desert. The cure was to look up at the bronze snake that Moses made. Similarly, worry is a human concept, and the cure is to look to God's precept—in this instance, the kingdom of God and his righteousness. And all the worries of life will be taken care of by God.

I have found that a praying person can intercede to Jesus and still not believe him. Multitudes love the Lord. They've given to people and served all their lives, yet they are dead broke and are struggling in life. I've often wondered about such people—they are good and kind and loving. They're treasures. Why do they suffer so much?

I've come to the realization that though they love Jesus with all their heart, they have lived their days believing human concepts and never fully experienced how to live according to the precepts of God. Their human concepts are their reality. Everybody lives in the world, but as Jesus said, we are in the world, but we are not *of* the world (John 17:16). What was he saying to us?

We are from another world.
We are from the world of God's precepts.

When the Word of God is spoken, it does not return void (Isaiah 55:11). A precept will always come to pass, whether it is through you or through somebody else. God wants it to come through you. But if you don't follow it and understand his precept, then it will be given to somebody else who will believe.

Bad Religion–The Conflict

Religion is the concept of humans. It was so powerful at one point that religious people prosecuted the God of the world and declared him guilty. Think about that. The Pharisees knew the written Word of God. But their entire philosophy and understanding of the Word of God was based on human concepts passed down through the generations through oral tradition. This is why the Pharisees could never accept the freedom Jesus brought. The kingdom brings freedom. Religion brings bondage.

The power of religion is stronger than that of demons. Demon spirits never troubled Jesus. When he entered a city, these demon spirits were petrified of him and they submitted to him, but the religious people wanted to kill him. The conflict between the precepts of God and the concepts of humans is the reason why we have bad religion.

Jesus Christ did not come to make a religion. He came to break a religion.

Because the concept of religion is so formal, so structured, so normal, it makes self-righteous people feel holy and morally superior. And it fits the box. So what happens when that box is deconstructed? I often joke at my events to show how wrong religion can be. For example, did you know that God would not be allowed to be a pastor in many of our churches because he's divorced? God gave a certificate of divorce to his bride, Israel. So, according to religion, God's not allowed to be a pastor. Think about that.

Religion keeps God away. It keeps him out. That's the power of a human concept. A person lifts up the Bible to people and says, "This is the Bible; this is what I think it's says. Now obey it." At a recent event, a couple said to me, "We have been happily married for two years. We started going to a church as we longed to be part of a family of fellow believers. We met with the pastor, who condemned us because we were both previously married and divorced. Religion refused to let us in."

Many times over, I have seen what the humanistic concept of religion has done to people. I do not waste my time fighting the devil because of Jesus he is too weak for me. Now the spirit of religion—that's a strongman. So, I pray, "Dear Lord, please keep me safe from your followers." (Joking.)

Hard Work Is an Enslaving Spirit

The religion of hard work has shaped our upbringing, culture, and environment. Therefore, we submit to the religion or curse of hard work and follow this spirit. Hard work is, in fact, a spirit—the spirit of mammon. The Lord Jesus clearly revealed it to the world.

> [Jesus] opened his mouth, and taught them, saying ... "No man can serve two masters: for either he will hate the one and love the other; or else he will hold to the one, and despise the other. Ye cannot serve God and mammon." (Matthew 6:24 KJV)

Here we see that there are two powerful gods in this world and humans can follow only one—either God the Father or the god called Mammon. Mammon is not money; it is the lust, greed, and insatiable appetite to get rich and have a selfish, materialistic lifestyle though a humanistic concept.

Mammon's title is Mammon-Ra—an ancient Syrian god of wealth, riches, and military might. Pharoah worshipped Mammon-Ra and was also called Mammon-Ra. Pharoah is a brutal and wicked ruler who enslaves people. As a slave master, he is a type of Satan on earth.

Mammon gives wealth to the world through hard work and wicked schemes, but God gives wealth to us, his children, because of what Jesus did for us. Let me put this another way: Jesus showed us how to get wealth and things *from God* by firstly seeking God's kingdom and righteousness. Jesus *never* told us to get wealth and things by being a slave to Mammon-Ra, also known as Pharoah.

3

MONEY MASTERY

You cannot live a life of unwork if you do not get the money part of life right.
If you get the money part right, you then get most of your life right.

Incorrect humanistic concepts have so infiltrated Christendom that we have made major financial errors. (I share more in the chapter "The Seven Financial Errors.")

I have often thought about the two most important things about money:

1. Why God gives money.
2. How God gives money.

WHY GOD GIVES MONEY

One day while in prayer, I heard a still small voice ask, "Why does God give money to his people?" and I replied with the classic Christian response, "To care for the poor and needy." But I heard the voice again say, "What did Jesus say in the parable of the ten talents?"

I found the parable in Luke 19 and studied it.

The Parable of the Talents

While they were listening to this, [Jesus] went on to tell them a parable, because he was near Jerusalem and the people thought that the kingdom of God was going to appear at once. He said: "A man of noble birth went to a distant country to have himself appointed king and then to return. So he called ten of his servants and gave them ten minas. 'Put this money to work,' he said, 'until I come back.'

"But his subjects hated him and sent a delegation after him to say, 'We don't want this man to be our king.'

"He was made king, however, and returned home. Then he sent for the servants to whom he had given the money, in order to find out what they had gained with it.

"The first one came and said, 'Sir, your mina has earned ten more.'

"'Well done, my good servant!' his master replied. 'Because you have been trustworthy in a very small matter, take charge of ten cities.'

"The second came and said, 'Sir, your mina has earned five more.'

"His master answered, 'You take charge of five cities.'

"Then another servant came and said, 'Sir, here is your mina; I have kept it laid away in a piece of cloth. I was afraid of you, because you are a hard man. You take out what you did not put in and reap what you did not sow.'

"His master replied, 'I will judge you by your own words, you wicked servant! You knew, did you, that I am a hard man, taking out what I did not put in, and reaping what I did not sow? Why then didn't you put my money on deposit, so that when I came back, I could have collected it with interest?'

"Then he said to those standing by, 'Take his mina away from him and give it to the one who has ten minas.'

"'Sir,' they said, 'he already has ten!'

"He replied, 'I tell you that to everyone who has, more will be given, but as for the one who has nothing, even what they have will be taken away. But those enemies of mine who did not want me to be king over them—bring them here and kill them in front of me.'"

— Luke 19:11–27

As I read through this parable, I was astonished at the many insights, but these five were highlighted:

1. **Trade**

God wants his children to do business and trade until he returns because the marketplace must be transformed by the kingdom of God through God's businesspeople. Our professional and business lifestyle of righteousness, peace, and joy in the Holy Spirit will impact the marketplaces for the glory of Jesus the King.

2. **Growth**

Money was given for the purpose of firstly making it grow and was not to be given away. We must not give away the seed (money); we must sow the seed in good investments. Out of the harvest, we are to give to the poor and needy, but we must also teach the poor and needy how to do the same.

We have a most unusual belief that when God gives us money, 90 percent belongs to us and ten percent belongs to him. And we live our merry lives giving 10 percent to him. However, this is not the case. When God gives us money, 100 percent of it belongs to him, and he requires us to grow it. So do not give back 10 percent; give him 110 percent. The best way I have found to grow God's money is to ask him. *Father, how do I grow your money?*

3. **Character**

God uses money to test our character and prove our trustworthiness. Money does not make us better or worse; it reveals who we truly are. The correct handling, growing, and managing of money is how he trains and equips us.

People who excel in good money management have excellent character and integrity. God himself can trust them (v. 10). God is in no hurry to build our character and make us rich. In fact, we are warned to not be greedy or in haste to become rich. Everything happens at the right time.

4. **Identity and Title**

God honors those who are wise with money. God loves all his children equally, but he gives more to those he trusts. One of the most astonishing things Jesus said was for us to use money to gain friends here on earth and that when we go home one day, we will be welcomed into high places in heaven (Luke 16:9). People who grow God's money wisely have an identity and the title of "good and faithful servant" on earth and in heaven.

5. **Authority**

God is looking to position his people in and over cities, but the qualification process is that they must first grow his money. Very clearly stated: A person who multiplies God's money receives the exact same percentage of authority over cities. If you multiply his money five times, you will receive authority over five cities. If you multiply it ten times, you will receive authority over ten cities. Doing good and great things gives us influence over others, but growing God's money gives us influence and authority in the spirit realm and the natural.

So, God gives us money so that we can learn the art of:

- ✓ making it grow,
- ✓ managing it, and
- ✓ multiplying it.

Those who master money can truly bring kingdom impact to the marketplace and the world.

HOW GOD GIVES MONEY

Several years after this revelation, I was on a cruise, crossing the Atlantic, and a thought entered my mind:

GOD DOES NOT GIVE MONEY TO HIS PEOPLE;
HE GIVES WISDOM *AND* PEOPLE *TO HIS PEOPLE.*

As I pondered the depth of this, I thought about my life and that of others, and then about my hero, the great man of faith George Muller—a man who cared for thousands of orphans and built orphanages for them in England; a man who received more than 100 million dollars from God through prayer. For Muller, money did not pour upon him like manna from heaven. It did not appear out of nowhere. It followed an intelligent design and pattern: George Muller had a *need*, God gave him *wisdom*, he *prayed*, then God sent him *people* who were aligned to his mission. *Through these people*, God transferred *all the money* that was needed.

My friend, here is the secret on how to get money God's way:

First, find out what God wants you to do and how much it is going to cost. (Remember, God is not obligated to finish what you started; he is obligated to finish what *he* started).

Second, ask God for wisdom, knowledge, understanding, insights, and instruction.

Third, ask him to align you with the right people for the mission. Sometimes they find you and sometimes, through his leading, you must go and find them.

Fourth, create a program or product or service and share it with clarity.

Fifth, receive the money.

4

THE SEVEN FINANCIAL ERRORS OF NICE CHRISTIANS

They don't submit to the Bible.

The seven financial errors of nice Christians have occurred repeatedly through the ages. We find these teachings on financial management in church history, but they are very unbiblical. When you take church teaching and place it against the Bible, church teaching must submit to the Bible. I'm going to expose these errors and eradicate them, so that you can flourish in the things of God.

Error #1— Money is evil.

We've heard it said all our lives; however, this is not true. You will not find that statement anywhere in the Bible. What the scripture says is, "The *love* of money is a root of all kinds of evil. Some people, eager for money, have wandered from the faith and pierced themselves with many griefs" (1 Timothy 6:10, emphasis added).

There are many roots of evil. The love of money is one of them. So, my friend, please understand that it is not money that is evil. The real root of all kinds of evil is when somebody *lusts* after money. Such a person is infected and affected by the god of this world, mammon.

Error #2— Money is not important.

Zig Ziglar used to joke that money is not the most important thing in the world, but that it's reasonably close to oxygen.

George Mueller—the mighty man of God, the man of faith to whom God gave more than 100 million dollars though prayer alone—often said, "Money is not important to God, but he knows it's important to man, therefore he gives it to us to get his work done." Hudson Taylor, a British Protestant Christian missionary to China, said, "God's work done God's way will never fail to receive God's resources."

Though money is not important to God, he gives us money to care for the practical needs of life, ministry, and business. The quickest way to stop a Christian ministry, a Christian business, or a church is to stop the cash flow. No matter how faithful people are, no matter how prayerful we are, we cannot feed anybody or care for anyone without the practical gift of money.

Error #3—Money is just a tool.

I am sure you have heard this before, but this declaration is nowhere in the Bible. It's not a biblical statement, philosophy, or belief. It is a quote by Ayn Rand, a devout atheist.

If you treat money as a hammer, like a tool in the garage, what respect do you have for money?

None.

We have borrowed a quote made by an atheist and speak as though it is a biblical doctrine. Money is not *a* tool. Money *buys* tools. Money is a gift given by God to people he trusts. God says in his Word that all the gold and all the silver belong to him. His gold and silver are not tools, they are gifts.

Error #4—Rich people cannot get into heaven.

Sorry Abraham, sorry Jacob and Isaac, sorry King David, sorry King Solomon, the richest man who ever lived. Religious conditioning tells us that if you are rich, you cannot make it into heaven. And religious people often quote the scripture about the rich young ruler, albeit incorrectly.

Let us take a closer look at this scripture.

> Jesus looked at him and loved him. "One thing you lack," he said. "Go, sell everything you have and give to the poor, and you will have treasure in heaven. Then come, follow me."
>
> At this the man's face fell. He went away sad, because he had great wealth.
>
> Jesus looked around and said to his disciples, "How hard it is for the rich to enter the kingdom of God!"
>
> The disciples were amazed at his words. But Jesus said again, "Children, how hard it is to enter the kingdom of God! It is easier for a camel to go through the eye of a needle than for someone who is rich to enter the kingdom of God."
>
> The disciples were even more amazed, and said to each other, "Who then can be saved?"
>
> Jesus looked at them and said, "With man this is impossible, but not with God; all things are possible with God."
>
> —Mark 10:21–27

The rich young ruler was a very interesting character, and we can learn much from this encounter between him and Jesus. The gospel writers describe him as being rich, young, and a ruler. None of these attributes disqualifies a person from entering the kingdom of God. There is a difference between "entering the kingdom of God" and salvation. Anyone who by faith believes Jesus, gives their heart to Jesus, and makes him the Lord and Savior of their life has been saved. They are born again and have received salvation, *not the kingdom*.

The kingdom of God is not salvation; it is righteousness, peace, and joy in the Holy Spirit; it is the government and rulership and kingship of Jesus Christ upon the earth. It has its own constitution. It is invisible and cannot be observed. It is the very presence of God within us. The kingdom is not one of talk but one of *power*.

The rich young ruler was a landowner and uber wealthy. This made him a lord of the land (landlord). He was obviously a public figure, a socialite. As a ruler, he was a man of influence and authority, a leader of the people. Jesus told him to "sell" his properties and possessions and give to the poor and to follow him. If the man sold all he owned, he still would have been young and still uber rich because Jesus did not tell him to *give* it all away. But the problem was that he would no longer be a lord of the land, or a socialite, or a ruler, or a man of influence. His identity would have changed from lord and ruler to disciple and follower of Jesus. The man's problem was in his ego and status and not his money. *His identity as a ruler was more important to him than being a follower*. His problem is no different from ours. What he lacked was humility, *and* he believed that he had to work and be good in order to inherit salvation and the kingdom.

Error #5—Good Christians must give all their money away.

I've met many a good Christian who has given all their wealth away and in old age, they have got nothing. I've seen this on the mission field too. This is amazing to me because it's contrary to what Scripture says: "Give, and it will be given to you. A good measure, pressed down, shaken together and running over, will be poured into your lap. For with the measure you use, it will be measured to you" (Luke 6:38).

The amount you give will determine the amount you get back. Remarkable, isn't it? The Bible teaches that when you give out of a cheerful heart, God gives you back more than you have given. So that is strange to me that you might consider giving all your money away—the gift God has given you—when the returning king was so angry with his servant for not investing his money. (Luke 19:11–27).

And one of the most shocking statements that I hear from nice Christians is when they talk about giving back to society. I dislike that phrase because if you are giving back to society, that begs the question: What did you take from society?

— Did you steal?
— Did you overcharge?
— Did you do something that was unrighteous?

Therefore, out of guilt, you now must give back. That's not biblical. We don't give back like that. Whatever we do, we do for Jesus and for people. When we trade or do business or work, we are instructed to work as though we are worshiping God. Yes, our work is a sweet incense of worship to our God.

We are to take the money (seed) God gives us and sow it, make it grow, and give with the right motives and a cheerful heart. Then God will give us back more than we could imagine.

Error #6—Tithe and God will give you cars, houses, and riches.

This is not the case.

When a person's motive is wrong, God will not give houses and cars and millions and billions just by you tithing to your church.

Yes, I do believe that God does give houses and cars and wealth to his people. I have met people whom God had given millions and billions, private jets, and yachts, and they are some of the most humble, generous, and godly people I know. However, they all received from God because they obeyed the Lord Jesus's instruction in Matthew 6: "Seek first his kingdom and his righteousness, and all these things will be given to you as well" (Matthew 6:33).

If a person's heart is not right before God, God will not give. If God is not priority number one, you can give all your money away, you can tithe all you have, and you will not receive because such a person's heart is materialistic, consumed by the stuff of the world.

Unfortunately, we find counterfeit people using Scripture to lie, manipulate, and control people to give them money. This is wrong and evil. It's a deviation from biblical truth. However, just because there's a counterfeit does not mean that there's no original. As a matter of fact, when you see a counterfeit, that's evidence that there is an original. The Mona Lisa has counterfeits and fakes all around the world, but the original is in the Louvre Museum in Paris.

The existence of counterfeit people doesn't take away from the fact that God does give great abundance to his people who seek first his kingdom and righteousness. When we seek his kingdom, we will receive kingdom rewards.

The Father knows what we need.

Error #7—Jesus was poor; therefore, Christians must be poor.

My friend, this is the foundational philosophy that is based on human wisdom and human understanding. It sounds nice but is unbiblical and flawed. I believe that it starts with the nativity scene plays many of us participated in as children—a scene that is, in fact, historically incorrect.

Let me explain. We see the nice little nativity scene where Mary and Joseph watch over the little baby Jesus in a manger. And then we see three men with either donkeys or camels around them. That is not the true picture of that night. And out of this has come so much unbiblical teaching. *Poor* little baby Jesus, born in a stable because he had *poor* parents. But Joseph and Mary were in the stable that night because—as Scripture clearly states—*there were no inns available.* There was not a single room available in the entire village. The hotels or the motels at that time had zero availability *because of the census. All* the people had to come back to Bethlehem. It wasn't because they didn't have money. Joseph was a carpenter and a tradesman. Carpenters were the technologists of their time, like the code writers of ours. They were smart people *and earned a good salary.*

By the time the magi reached the baby Jesus, he would have been about two years old. He was not in a manger in Bethlehem. He was home in Nazareth approximately 90 miles away. Nowhere in Scripture does it say that three men came, or three magi, or three kings. It only says they brought three types of gifts.

Now here's the remarkable thing. Peter J. Daniels, the Christian billionaire, commissioned a team of historians to find out just how much wealth the magi brought to the baby Jesus. It was discovered that *more than three hundred kings* had come bearing gifts for Jesus, with a calculated wealth of more than *four million dollars* in today's standards. Persian documents showed that the gifts were escorted by an army.

> This Parthian delegation was offering tribute money to a 'king,' and therefore would more likely have brought a whole train of pack animals loaded with gold, frankincense and myrrh . . .
>
> The Parthians regarded Jesus as royalty, and it was the ancient custom to give a royal personage a truly worthy gift when coming into his presence.
>
> Since the Parthian Magi were directed to Jesus by an angel of God, their sense of awe likely resulted in unusually large gifts being given to Jesus.
>
> —Stephen Collins, *The Lost Ten Tribes of Israel… Found!*

And the reference in Matthew 2:3 regarding Herod and the people being troubled was because they thought Jesus's gift bearers were an invading army. Joseph and Mary had to flee Egypt and stay there because Herod was killing boys under two years of age. The family would have needed lots of money to leave their home, make the dangerous trip, and then settle in a foreign country, Egypt.

God is the God of wisdom. He is a God who takes care of every little thing. Jesus said to his disciples, "When you were with me, did you have need for anything?" Jesus even had a treasurer (Judas). People around Jesus gave money to Jesus. Jesus was not a poor person as taught to us by religious conditioning. When we study the Scriptures ourselves, we can clearly see how very practical God truly is.

These are the seven financial errors that are made by nice Christians. These things have distorted the truth and how we think about money. The average Christian person is financially illiterate. And most Christian leaders are not qualified to teach about financial wealth because they've been taught incorrectly about money. Money is not a tool. Money is a gift from God given to people whom he trusts, and money must be respected the way we respect all other gifts given to us by God.

5

FREEDOM FROM POVERTY

Rest for hard work.

All through my life, I worked hard. I was always the superstar—top sales producer, most liked, hardest worker—and I almost always won every sales competition due to my work ethic and drive. Yes, this meant working sixteen to eighteen hours a day. That's no rest and no life.

I was very proud of my achievements. Every president and CEO I ever worked for liked me. I found myself at their private events, and even dinners at their homes, where I met their families and friends. But I was most impressed when I spoke to their kids.

The conversations usually went something like this:

> Me: So, Johnny, what are you going to do when you grow up?
>
> Johnny: I will run my daddy's company.
>
> Me: So, Beth, what are you going to do when you grow up?
>
> Beth: Mum and Dad want me to study business in Europe as we plan to establish a global presence.
>
> Me: So, Scott, what are you going to do when you grow up?

> Scott: I want to be an investor, so my parents are sending me to ABC Investment University.

One day it hit me:

> *Poor people* teach their children how to be an excellent employee, work hard for somebody else, and retire with a little bit of money.
>
> *Rich people* teach their children how to work smart, be the boss, and have money working for them *forever*.

I knew my problem. Even though I was successful, I had the poverty rope on my life. Let me explain.

The Poverty Rope

In my mid-thirties I was very successful, yet I was still bound. I was travelling the world, speaking at business events, and preaching. It was then I realized that success and money do not remove poverty. Poverty is not just the lack of money; it is also a lethal rope of three strands:

1. The *spirit* of poverty
2. The poverty *mentality*
3. The *curse* of poverty

People who grew up in poverty or who are poor still carry poverty until God deals with them, as he did with me soon after, when I had my moment that completely changed my destiny. My wife Michele and I were travelling to Israel and, as usual, I booked a cheap, three-star hotel and economy flights. It was an unusually long trip with many connections, which is often the case with cheap tickets. On a connecting flight, my body was in pain; I was tired and a bit upset. As I walked down the aisle through first class and business class, making my way to the cheap seats at the back, I cried out to God, thinking, *Father, I am your child and I am here doing your will. My body is sore and I am in pain. Why do I have to sit in this uncomfortable seat in economy class while all these other people in first and business class get to rest and relax and sleep in their seats that turn into beds,*? Immediately I heard the voice of God say to me, *Who told you to book an economy seat? I will meet you at whatever level you want me to.*

We reached Jerusalem, Israel, and checked into our cheap hotel. It was awful. Michele said that we should check out of the hotel. I disagreed, but she was not happy. So, I asked her where she'd want to stay. She pointed to a beautiful five-star hotel called the King David. I laughed and said, "Do you have any idea how much a room costs at a five-star hotel?" Well, there are moments in life, and especially in marriage, when you know you are going to lose. This was one of those moments. We called a cab and checked in at the King David.

Oh yes. It was expensive.

The cost was no problem for Michele, but while she enjoyed testing the complementary snacks and chocolates, I had to go for a walk to clear my mind.

What I am about to say will resonate with most people who grew up with nothing. When I started to be financially successful, I had no problem blessing others. I would buy people gifts and the best foods and send them on vacations; however, I could never justify spending money on myself. My thought was *Let me eat cheap and stay at cheap places, so that I can give the extra money to the poor, orphans, and widows.*

As I walked around the King David hotel, I found myself in the main lobby where, for some reason, I felt urged to look down. On the floor tiles were the names and signatures of all the famous people who had stayed there. I recognized most names, but I came to a name that made me stop—Billy Graham. I promptly burst into tears. I heard the voice of God deep inside me say, *He is my ambassador and so are you. You belong here.* Something like a thick chain snapped inside me. I felt the atmosphere change, and I could breathe with such ease compared to how I'd felt leaving our expensive hotel room. Everything around me looked so different. My back straightened, and I walked through the crowds of people in the lobby with a brand-new sense of freedom and authority. Poverty had finally let go of me.

Today, years later, we travel in first and business class and stay in luxury hotels. God takes care of us. And yes, I am still able to abundantly bless the poor, orphans, and widows.

Poverty Preachers

Every now and then I get a person who asks me, "Melvin, are you a prosperity preacher?" I jokingly respond, "Are you a poverty preacher?"

I've ministered in leper communities, where one can smell the very stench of rotting human flesh. I've seen humans crawl like animals, dragging themselves on their bellies because their leprosy has eaten their limbs. I've seen people pick grains of rice from the floor, dust out the dirt, and then eat it because each grain meant the difference between life and death. I have ministered in refugee camps and seen babies' limbs torn apart by landmines, and men and women's bodies riddled by bullet holes; people crying out for death instead of living another day with no food and no hope. No, my friend, poverty is not the way that any human should live. Not anybody made in the image of God.

I do not believe that everybody is going to be a multimillionaire; however, I do believe that everybody should live a life that's prosperous.

I believe that the biblical definition of prosperity is "freedom from poverty." I want to see people freed of poverty. And so, we all should live in prosperity, not just having our needs met but also our wants met, because of this great verse in Psalm 23:1: "The Lord is my shepherd, I lack nothing." The ESV translates it as "The LORD is my shepherd; I shall not want." God not only meets our needs; he also provides our wants.

Giving Beyond Needs = Encouragement

I was a missionary for a long time, travelling to some of the hardest unreached places on earth. I have found that when you supply the *needs* of a missionary, you help them to continue the work, but when you supply their *wants*, you encourage their hearts. On the mission field, I used to take missionaries out for a nice lunch, or I would buy them clothing. I'd often buy their children chocolates or something sweet, a little extra—not just their needs but something they really wanted. I can tell you with much joy that when you provide for a missionary's wants, you find something different—they get extremely encouraged.

Meeting the needs of people keeps them going but granting the wants of people keeps them encouraged.

That's why God gives us our wants as well as our needs. Freeing people from poverty is why I believe we should be prosperous and why we must speak the message that the Lord has given us to set people free from a life of poverty.

Poverty Is Evil

I guess we can all relate to moments of being broke and even poor, but poverty is unlike anything on earth. It is an oppression and an evil. Poverty is not just the lack of money, it is *a mentality, a curse, and a spirit.* It attaches itself to a family and is passed down from generation to generation. I have found this to be true. Whatever parents do in moderation, their children will do in abundance. I have seen the blessings of righteous, humble parents pass on to their children a hundredfold. I have seen the curses, sin, and hatred of wicked parents pass on to their children a hundredfold. And the snowball effect of hard work and poverty grows from generation to generation.

The Lord Jesus said the poor we will always have with us (Matthew 26:11), but he never said that about poverty. In this world of ours, we have those who are broke, those who are poor, those who live in poverty, those who live in prosperity, and those who live in abundance. I believe that everybody should live in prosperity, meaning having their needs and wants taken care of and having the freedom from the poverty mentality, the curse of poverty, and the spirit of poverty.

Prosperity is for all who are made in the image of God. The abundance of God is given to a select group of God's people. God loves all his children, but *he gives the abundance to those he trusts.* Godly people who live in abundance are God's conduits on earth, the ones who know how to grow his money and are generous to the needy, not only giving money but—just as importantly—teaching people how to *grow* God's money. These are the millionaires and billionaires and trillionaires of God.

> Unwork *helps to change the poverty mentality, break the curse of poverty, and cast out the spirit of poverty.*

Freedom from Human Concepts

Precious are the thoughts of God about us. His thoughts about us are absolutely beautiful. His precepts about us are astonishing. But the way we think about ourselves is shocking. I think we all should take some time to release, destroy, and crush all humanistic concepts about ourselves. (Wrong thinking, negative thinking, and cynicism are symptoms of humanistic concepts.) A humanistic concept is in direct opposition of God's precept. It is trying to say that God is wrong. It's trying to say that God's Word is limited. It opposes the gospel of Jesus Christ.

When I was a new believer, I often asked the Lord this question: "Lord! King David did such nasty things. Why did you call him a man after your own heart. In contrast, the disciples only doubted. And Jesus rebuked them."

And then God said about David, "After removing Saul, he made David their king. God testified concerning him: 'I have found David son of Jesse, a man after my own heart; he will do everything I want him to do'" (Acts 13:22). David understood the precepts of God and did everything the precept told him to do, while the disciples never understood the precepts of Jesus, even though they had Jesus in their midst. And that's why Jesus constantly rebuked them.

At my events, I have often said to my audience that I believe the disciples didn't believe a word Jesus said. And I ask them these questions:

— Did Jesus say that he was the Son of God.

— Yes!

— Did Jesus say that he would be put to death ?

— Yes!

— Did Jesus say that he would be resurrected in three days?

— Big YES!

— How many disciples turned up on the morning of his resurrection with breakfast?
— None!

A few women showed up with spices for the dead body.

Not a single disciple believed him.

The disciples did not believe God's precepts, unlike David, who understood God's precepts. Therefore, even in his imperfections, God still trusted him. This was a man after God's own heart. The man was an adulterer, a murderer, a liar. If you long with all your heart to know God's precepts, God honors you. What a shocking thing. You can be the worst type of person, but God honors a man or a woman who honors his precepts.

I am sure most of us know nonbelievers who seem closer to God than some people who go to church because these nonbelievers have reverence for God. It's like that little fable told of the rabbi and a prostitute who lived across from his house:

> Every morning the rabbi would get up and faithfully do his rituals and prayer. He would then look across the street at the house of the prostitute and think about all the nasty things she would have done the night before, and he would say, "God, thank you that I'm not like that woman." And the prostitute would get up in the morning and look across the street at the house of the rabbi and cry out, "God, please make me like that man, a man of God."

Some people have not been to Sunday school and not been to church, yet they have more respect for the Word of God than people who sit in church and hear the beautiful Word of God over and over and over again.

Rid Yourself

Friend,

— What are some human concepts of religion in you?
— What are some human concepts that have been formed in your mind about who you are?
— What are some human concepts of the world that have entered you?

Are there human concepts you have lived out and shared with other people? They may sound nice, but they are limited and often place you in bondage. Perhaps it's time for you to let go and crush these concepts right now.

Take a few minutes and write them down, pray over them, and rid yourself of them once and for all.

I had a wrong concept about the world of politics. And because of that wrong concept, I was not ministering to that group of people. My concept was my roadblock. One day I said, "God, forgive me for this incorrect human concept because the precept says that God places kings in office. And when a nation goes astray, God will allow an ungodly leader in a position of power, so that the people can be corrected and humble their hearts (1 Peter 2:14). Lord, teach me your precepts and let them take over." A few weeks later I received a call from an ambassador who connected me to several leaders. Within a few months, I was positioned in Washington D.C. and working with diplomats and leaders from several nations. God opened doors for me to be an advisor to influential leaders.

The most remarkable thing was that two decades earlier, I received prophetic words from dozens of different people that I would be working with world leaders. It never came to pass. And honestly, I'd been rebuking the devil for a long time, praying and hoping, but nothing happened until I removed my human concept; then everything happened.

My friend, what are the human concepts that are the roadblocks in your life? The things that stop you?

A friend of mine shared this story.

> She was fifty years old and single. Her heart's desire was to be married, but it never happened. Her concept was that she would never be a good wife because she was a strong leader. She was told that strong women were like Jezebels and that she should never marry because she would never be able to submit and would always control her husband. She believed these concepts all her life. Then one day she chose to look at the precepts of God regarding marriage and, after some time, she dealt with the human concepts. Within a few years, she married. This dear lady prayed and fasted for more than twenty-five years and nothing happened, yet when she dealt with the human concepts, the promise came to pass.

Human concepts are so powerful and destructive that they enter the mind and become stumbling blocks and roadblocks. I think about the well-known biblical story of when Peter used human concepts and tried to obstruct the Lord by saying that Jesus would never be crucified, and Jesus replied to Peter by saying, "Get behind me, Satan! You are a stumbling block to me" (Matthew 16:23), and told Peter that he had in his mind the wisdom (human concepts) of man and not the wisdom of God (God's precepts).

Prayer to Free Yourself from Human Concepts

Lord Jesus, ever since I was a child, I was taught human concepts, but you said that one must come to you as a child because a child can understand kingdom precepts much more easily than an adult. I ask that every human concept that has been a stumbling block and roadblock in my life be removed, crushed, and destroyed now, in the mighty name of Jesus. I thank you that I am now free from human concepts. Please teach me your precepts, so that I will meditate on your wonderful works. I will live in the goodness of God all the days of my life. Amen.

6

THE PROPHESY AND BLUEPRINT OF THE CURSE OF HARD WORK

Prophecies and blueprints go hand in hand: A prophecy says what will happen and a blueprint shows how it will happen.

There is power in prophecy. Much of the trouble we face is because of a prophecy we have spoken. We call this a self-fulfilling prophecy. Thoughts and words set the stage for success or failure.

Remember our friend Job? He was the most righteous and greatest man on the earth, yet there was one little thing that caused him much sorrow, and it was a human concept.

Job said:

> "What I always feared has happened to me.
> What I dreaded has come true.
>
> I have no peace, no quietness.
> I have no rest; only trouble comes." (Job 3:25–26 NLT)

The power of your thought will make a heaven or a hell for your life. There was no one more righteous on earth at that time than Job. He was wise, he was powerful, but he had one flaw. Fear was suppressed deep inside his mind and heart. He was afraid of something, and his fear became his prophecy which became his reality.

It's important to know that your fearful thoughts will lead to fearful emotions, which lead to fearful words. Have you ever said something in fear and then caught yourself and thought, *I cannot believe I said that*? That's the inner demon, the enemy inside your brain. It is so small and often overlooked, and it will destroy you. My friend, remember this: Giants don't trip over mountains; they trip over pebbles.

The apostle Paul warned us to not create a loophole for the enemy to exploit. The loophole becomes the legal right. The legal right is the word or the sentence you speak. In this instance, the loophole and legal right are what we have created our identity around—the false prophesy of hard work.

We Proudly Proclaim, "I Am a Hard Worker."

A thought of hard work becomes an emotion of hard work, which becomes words of hard work, which ultimately become a life of hard work. It's because of the prophecy spoken over us ever since we were conceived that we work so hard and cannot be free from the shackles of life.

Words are not meaningless; they bring either life or death. We are where we are and what we are because of the prophecy and the blueprint of the curse of hard work. The reason why people work so hard is because it has been prophesied over them as children. When we were still in our mother's womb, we learned about hard work.

Hard work is the biggest lie, the biggest killer, the biggest god in this world. It has killed millions, enslaved billions, and robbed more marriages and families than any other system since the garden of Eden. Most of us can relate to growing up in an environment that has taught us the prophecy of hard work.

There are seven prophetic humanistic concepts that were spoken over us as children. The words may be spoken differently in your house, but the concepts are the same:

> #1 My child, work hard in school so that you can get good grades and go to college.
>
> #2 My child, work hard in college so that you can get good grades and get a good job.
>
> #3 My child, work hard at your job so that you will earn good money and get married.
>
> #4 My child, marriage is tough, but you must work hard at your marriage.
>
> #5 My child, have children of your own, but keep in mind children are hard work.
>
> #6 My child, work hard to be a good parent so you can give your children the best.

> #7 My child, do not talk to strangers and do not ask for money; work hard, be nice to everyone, and teach your children to do the same.

Like sheep going to the slaughter, we unwittingly follow these unwritten laws of life, ensnared by their vicious cycles and drudgery. And with pinpoint accuracy, the prophecy is fulfilled in our lives—we are saddled from generation to generation with the curse of hard work.

School became hard work and college became hard work. Our job became hard work. Our marriage became hard work. Our children became hard work. We did not talk to strangers and missed all the great opportunities God had for us. We did not ask for money and missed all the additional sales and pay raises that were rightfully ours. We worked hard and became nice people, timid and plagued by the fear of rejection, fear of failure, and fear of what other people think of us.

Then somewhere around the age of sixty-five to seventy, we are told that we are now too old and it's time to retire, give up on our dreams, and get ready to die.

And not once did we ask the question *why!*

> Why must school be hard work?
>
> Why must college be hard work?
>
> Why must my job be hard work?
>
> Why must my marriage be hard work?
>
> Why must my children be hard work?
>
> Why must my life be hard work?

True are the words of the adage: There are none so blind as those who will not see. We will not see because we cannot see, we cannot see because we have no insight, and we have no insight because we have the wrong concept of life and work—because we do not understand *God's* precepts for our life and work.

That's the prophecy and, in my opinion, the chief enemy we are fighting against. Hard work sounds so right. It sounds so nice, so noble; but, my friend, it is the chief enemy that you will face, and the world is under the curse of this prophecy. Jesus said the god of this world is mammon. And even more alarming, these seven prophecies are the attributes of mammon. Unfortunately, we are shackled to this curse since the day we were born, through kindergarten, through school, through college, through work, and until death. And many are the times we have prophesied this curse over our children, family, friends, and teams. There is nothing good and nothing true about hard work. And we are going to learn about this and understand why this curse must be broken.

These are not mere words. They are in opposition to what the Lord wants for us. When we oppose what God wants, it is called disobedience and rebellion.

— Hard work is disobedience.
— Hard work is rebellion.
— Hard work is you rejecting what God wants for you.
— Hard work is a curse.

The Worst Words

Let's go a bit further. We received these prophecies of the curse of hard work from our parents and elders. Now, I'm not blaming our parents; I am not saying that they were bad. They taught us what they knew. We must honor our parents, but we must also carefully evaluate their wisdom. I often joke that the Bible says to the wife to honor her husband, but it does not say to honor the devil in him.

Parents, elders, and mentors can sometimes give the worst human concepts. It is my opinion that most parents do not fully realize that after the heavenly Father's blessing, the next most powerful blessing over a child's life is the blessing from the mouths of their parents. Sadly, many parents unknowingly speak curses over their children's lives and destinies.

7

THE TEN PRECEPTS OF WORK

There is a profound difference between work and hard work.

Hard work is a humanistic concept. Work is a kingdom precept. Hard work is connected to the curse of Genesis 3.

[God] said to the man, "You listened to your wife and ate fruit from the tree, although I commanded you, 'You must never eat its fruit.'

The ground is cursed because of you.

Through hard work you will eat food that comes from it every day of your life.

The ground will grow thorns and thistles for you,
and you will eat wild plants.

By the sweat of your brow, you will produce food to eat
until you return to the ground,
because you were taken from it.
You are dust, and you will return to dust."
—Genesis 3:17-19 (GW).

Hard work is warfare, and people have to fight for survival, therefore we call it the hustle or the grind, and use idioms like "blood, sweat, and tears," or "backs to the grindstone," and "burning the candle at both ends." It's what I call being a conqueror. But God calls us to be more than conquerors. This illustration will elaborate my point a bit more.

The Two Boxers

Two heavyweight boxers were fighting for the title of Heavyweight Champion of the World. Both were formidable fighters. They went after each other; round after round they battled. Through the pain and the toil, the blood, the sweat, and the tears, they fought for their bread. Finally, the faster man struck the other on the jaw and knocked him out. The crowd cheered and the bell rang. The referee announced the winner by total knockout (TKO). They placed the check in the hands of the winner; he was the conqueror. He went home and placed the check in his wife's hands; she was more than the conqueror.

Our greatest victories come from the battles we do not fight.

- — The curse of hard work is the burden given to those who must battle as conquerors.
- — The privilege of work is given to those who are more than conquerors.

Hard work is you fighting *for* victory. Work is you resting *in* God's victory.

The Law of First Mention says that to understand a particular word or set of beliefs, we must find the first place in Scripture that word or belief is revealed and study that passage. The first time work is mentioned in the Bible is Genesis 2:3:

> By the seventh day God had finished the work he had been doing; so on the seventh day he rested from all his work. Then God blessed the seventh day and made it holy, because on it he rested from all the work of creating that he had done.
>
> — Genesis 2:2–3

God rested from work. So, rest is the finished work of God. And a closer look reveals that God worked six days, and when he was finished, he blessed the seventh day of rest and *not* the six days of work. This leads me to ask the question that if God rested from work, what *is* work?

Work has nothing to do with the nine-to-five or the hustle or grind. It is blasphemy to think that God went to work the way humans go to work because his ways are not our ways.

Work is an action, a dynamic, a force. Therefore, faith without action is dead.

PRECEPT ONE – GOD CREATED

You do not *go* to work because if you are thinking, you are working. Instead of going to work, you should go to rest.

"In the beginning God created the heavens and the earth" (Genesis 1:1). The first precept is to create. The first thing you must do as work is create something. It has nothing to do with going into the office.

What do you create?
A thought.

Everything that is around you, each thing that your eyes see, was first a creative thought in somebody's mind. You are here because your parents thought about each other and, more importantly, because God thought about you. Your thoughts are powerful. Your thoughts create something.

How you think leads to how you feel, which leads to how you speak, which leads to how you practice, which leads to how you perform, which become your habits, which determine success or failure.

We are designed to think, therefore we are always creating good things or bad things. Good thoughts create good things and toxic thoughts create bad things.

The first thing God did was create.

The first thing I do every morning is ask God for a thought. I call it a "kingdom power thought." Sometimes it's a word. Sometimes it's a sentence. I think deeply about it and allow it to become a creative thought. Over the years these have become the bedrock of all my business dealings and have brought me tremendous rewards.

I guess we will never know how many inventions are lost in the shower every morning. A lady once told me her great grandfather was an entrepreneur, and God gave him the thought of "moving stairs." Unfortunately, her great grandfather did not do anything with that thought. And a short while later, in 1892, Jesse Reno patented his moving stairs.

Your first action is to think and create thoughts. God gives creative thoughts to people, but most people are too busy working to pay attention. We can solve all our personal, national, and international problems if we would just think and create.

PRECEPT TWO – GOD HOVERED

"The Spirit of God was hovering over the waters" (Genesis 1:2). To hover has a slightly negative connotation to it. It means to be so close to something that you are almost controlling it. You are extremely possessive and are consumed by it. You are protective of your thoughts; you are guarding them from the enemy. In other words, you are focused intensely, like a laser.

Laser Like Focus

So, what did God do? The first thing he did was create the thought and then he hovered over what he created. The second thing you must do when you have a creative thought is hover over it and ask yourself, *Is this a good thought or a toxic thought*?

When I was newly married, my wife Michele would see me sitting in a corner rolled up in a ball. One day she mustered up the courage to ask what I was doing, and I replied, "I am working." After many years together, she said to me, "You are hovering over a thought, aren't you?" I asked how she knew this, and she replied that she could see the smoke coming out of my ears.

Most of us do not hover over our creative thoughts. And as a result, we have formed the bad habit of having just fleeting thoughts. Have you ever felt God drop something in your mind that is very good, but within a few short moments you say to yourself, *Oh, come on, stop being so childish. Stop being so foolish. It will never happen, not for me anyway*. What have you just done? You have thrown away the second precept of work. And you get stuck in the grind, in the hard work.

Here's the pattern to follow: get the creative thought and then hover over it. Don't let go of it. Grab it. Sit with it. Chew on that thought. Because you are working. You truly are.

Leadership expert John Maxwell has got an amazing philosophy. He has a chair he sits on and thinks in. He calls it his thinking chair. A story is told of a new employee who joined an organization. He was a close relative of the CEO. Every day he walked past an office with its door open and noticed a man sitting and staring out the window. The new guy decided to complain about him to the boss, but to his surprise, the boss responded by saying, "Don't you dare interrupt him. Last year one of his ideas made us several million dollars."

Microsoft once conducted a study and discovered that the average attention span of an adult is eight seconds, while the attention span of a goldfish is nine. We have formed a bad habit of not focusing or hovering over thoughts. But we can change, and we can grow. We can hover because it's work.

PRECEPT THREE – GOD SPOKE

"God said, 'Let there be light,' and there was light" (Genesis 1:3). Jesus is the living Word, and there is power in our words.

A scientist friend of mine told me about studies conducted by Mr. Masaru Emoto, who started freezing water in 1994 and taking photographs of resultant crystals. In one study he took two containers of water and spoke over container 1, adding positive words like "love" and "gratitude," and over container 2 he spoke negative words like "you are stupid" and "you are useless." The results were astonishing. Container 1 had beautiful, perfect crystals but container 2's water had produced deformed, misshaped crystals.

Thoughts and Emotions

Leading neurologists say a thought has a corresponding emotion. And Jesus said that out of the fullness (emotion) of the heart, a person will speak (Luke 6:45).

Our words are work and our words go to work.

God spoke what he felt, and God felt what he thought.

God thinks -> God feels -> God speaks

During the time of creation, the earth was covered by water. The sound of God's words produced light, and it's important to note that this light was not from the sun but was most likely produced out of water. Think about it: this light was spoken into existence on day 1, and *the sun and moon only came into existence on day 4.*

One of the most fascinating properties of water is called sonoluminescence, which is when light emerges out of sound. Soundwaves trap small bubbles within water, making them shrink, expand, and give off a flash of light. So if the human body is made up of approximately 60 percent water, the sound of your words becomes light inside you. This light carries energy, force, and power. It shines out of you and affects things around you. Your words bring life and hope and transformation. As Jesus said, "You are the light of the world" (Matthew 5:14).

One Man's Words

In 2001 I moved from South Africa to New Zealand. I got a job as a salesman selling home security alarms. I struggled to sell many, and eventually got kicked out of the boarding house because I could not afford my rent. Things were extremely difficult. Now homeless, I slept in the boardroom of the sales company. One day I was out knocking on doors, trying to sell something, and I found myself at a public library. I sensed a prompting to go inside, so I did and found an audiocassette tape titled "See You at the TOP" by Zig Ziglar. It cost two dollars to rent, and I chose to rent it instead of buying lunch.

The sound of Zig Ziglar's voice and words were filled with energy, force, and power. I was stirred, inspired, and encouraged, newly filled with hope and excitement. His words were light to me and removed all the darkness in my thoughts. He made me feel that I could achieve the impossible. True are the words of Carl W.

fuel light was on, and I was broke. My rented Zig Ziglar cassette tape kept playing, and as Mr. Ziglar ended with his ever-popular signature, "And I will see you at the TOP!" I saw myself on the platforms of the world. I heard myself speak and I felt the buzz of the audience. With insight I could see, with intelligence I could articulate, and with intuition I could project my feelings. Years later, my thoughts became my reality.

The Wisdom of an Ant

More than 3,000 years ago, King Solomon, the wisest and wealthiest man that ever lived, said,

> Go to the ant, ...
> consider its ways and be wise!
> It has no commander,
> no overseer or ruler,
> yet it stores its provisions in summer
> and gathers its food at harvest.
> (Proverbs 6:6–8)

That is remarkable. Solomon saw the ant and watched its ways. He observed with intensity and curiosity, and he was challenging us to do the same.

In order for us to *see*, let us consider this little creature called an ant and observe some of its amazing ways, so that we can use this wisdom in our lives. An ant is the only creature apart from a human that farms its food.

An ant functions in three specific ways:

1. An ant functions through insight.
2. An ant functions through intelligence.
3. An ant functions through intuition.

Insight, intelligence, and intuition—a three-in-one package that makes the ant such a successful creature. Consider how the ant has been created: an ant has no ears, and many species of ants don't have eyes, and so the ant cannot see, nor can it hear. This leads us to conclude that the ant only functions through insight, intuition, and intelligence. The ant's supernatural ability called insight is what makes the ant successful, not its ability to see where it is going.

It's important to note that you don't have to always see everything. You don't have to always hear. As a matter of fact, the less you see with your eyes and hear, the better for you. The world is full of negativity, but the ant cannot see or hear the negativity and the criticism from the outside world. Similarly, when God gives you insight and tells you to do something, *do not listen* to negativity. *Do not listen* to those who tell you that you can't do it.

What We Project

The ant lives on its ability to recognize danger and to recognize opportunities, and when it encounters either, the ant functions by producing and giving off a chemical called pheromones that other ants pick up on. Likewise, humans give off "psychological projection." We project our feelings. Our psychological projection will get us into places that we might have previously deemed impossible.

Our psychological projection contains all our beliefs and philosophy, which are inside us and projected from within without our even saying a word. Therefore, our philosophy in life has to be positive and good.

Your ability to create a successful life has got very little to do with the economy and everything to do with the right philosophy.

Make Thinking Your Work

The ant was designed for success. An ant can lift between ten to fifty times its own weight, is said to be the strongest creature in proportion to size than any other living creature, is very quick, and can chew at 140 miles per hour. Some species can lift a hundred times their own weight.

Just like ants, we humans are designed to take on more than we think we can. When it comes to thinking, it is said that we only use 10 percent of our thinking ability. We *can* think more, we *can* think deeper. We *can* think longer. We *can* think better. I love the philosophy of the British Special Air Service (SAS): Train Hard, Fight Easy. My philosophy is, Think Deep, Work Light.

We can think more than we currently think. We can also think deeper.

Make thinking your work. Spend more time thinking deeper, longer, wider, and further. This is your work—to think like the ant. You have been designed for success.

Research shows that the more you think, the more intelligent you become. Neuroscientists say that when you think about a specific thing for at least seven minutes, you gain better understanding of it. You grow better, stronger, firmer thoughts. Your thought life becomes much sounder. And you indeed become more intelligent the more you think about a certain thing.

When insight, intelligence, and intuition come together, you can truly envision and see the reality of your amazing thoughts.

PRECEPT FIVE - GOD DIVIDED

"He separated the light from the darkness" (Genesis 1:4). Separating the old from the new, the weak from the strong, and the bad from the good at the right time is wise.

It is exhilarating to watch a space rocket launch. At an altitude of approximately twenty-four nautical miles, the boosters separate from the orbiter or external tank, descend on parachutes, and land in the ocean, where they are then recovered and refurbished. This is their cycle of life. Successful rocket launches into outer space always have a separation at the right time.

Our work of separation is key to a successful life. We must be vigilant. Weeds must be separated from grass, sheep must be separated from goats, and so, too, must good thoughts be separated from bad thoughts. Not all ideas work, and not all thoughts will be fruitful. Dividing and separating can be painful, especially when dealing with people and loved ones, but it is vital for our growth. Separating is our work.

When your project reaches a certain point, it's time to divide, separate, and remove things or people. The worst thing to do is to keep people on when they're not supposed to be on. And at times you must let go of some clients. It is very often the case that holding on to even the right people at the wrong time will cause you to miss what God has for you. If you keep people on that are not supposed to be on, they'll weigh you down. Your work of sifting through is what will ensure that your work stays as work and does not become hard work.

Most of our hard work has to do with the wrong people in our midst.

Pruning

Cutting off and pruning is important for a life of fruitfulness.

> "I am the true vine, and my Father is the gardener. He cuts off every branch in me that bears no fruit, while every branch that does bear fruit he prunes so that it will be even more fruitful." (John 15:1–2)

A client of mine, I will call him John, was locked in a noncompete contract with his business partner. This partner of his was a very difficult person, and although the money was good, he made life a living hell on earth for John. I coached John over a five-year period, and every time he asked what to do about his business partner, we came to the same conclusion: separate yourself, cut your losses, and start your own business. But John was caught in the classic "freedom vs the unknown" scenario. He would rather suffer and endure the pain than walk away because at least he knew what to expect. Then the time came for me to separate from John. A few years later I received an email from John saying that he'd finally done it and was now pursuing a totally different path. Today John runs his own successful international business and is also a senior government official. It is predicated that he will soon become the president of his country.

The work of dividing and separating is very important because everything in its natural state will eventually break down, decay, and rot. But the regenerative process works because things are cut off, pruned, and removed. Even the branches of trees that are cut off and thrown to the ground have a purpose—they help the process and cycle of growth. So never be disheartened by the separating process. *Nothing is wasted with God.*

PRECEPT SIX - GOD CALLED

"God called the light 'day,' and the darkness he called 'night.' And there was evening, and there was morning—the first day" (Genesis 1:5).

What you are called becomes your calling.

There's a difference between naming something and calling something. For example, your parents named you and people now call you by your name. However, God does not call you by your name; he calls you by your identity, which is your divine purpose. Therefore, the Lord Jesus said to the disciples that he would no longer *call* them his servants but instead he *called* them his friends. This is because what you are called becomes your calling.

Our work is to call our project into being—to call its existence and proclaim its destiny. We see in the Bible that God frequently renamed and called people into their callings. In Judges 6 we read the story of Gideon, who, by his own definition, belonged to the weakest clan and was the least of his entire family. He was hiding and threshing wheat because he was afraid of the enemy the Midianites. However, God called him by his identity and destiny. Gideon was called "mighty hero," and he became exactly what God called him to be. "The angel of the LORD appeared to him and said, 'Mighty hero, the LORD is with you!'" (Judges 6:12).

When you call a thing by its destiny, you have given it permission to succeed.

A famous baseball player once said that on one occasion, he was asked to speak at a prison to hardened criminals. His keynote topic was "I Am What My Father Said I Would Be." He proceeded to tell the story of how as a little boy his dad would call him "champ" and said, "Someday you will be a famous sportsman." After the player's speech, he walked down the corridor of cells and stopped by one man to greet him. "Sir," the prisoner said, "I am also the man my father said I would become. My father called me "convict" and said, "Someday you will end up in prison."

What you call your business, your projects, and yourself will truly become reality. Adam was given the privilege of calling and naming each living creature. Surely, he named each one by what he *saw* the creature do and was called to do.

> Now the LORD God had formed out of the ground all the wild animals and all the birds in the sky. He brought them to the man to see what he would name them; and whatever the man called each living creature, that was its name. (Genesis 2: 19)

"The two most important days in a person's life are the day you are born and the day you find out why."
(Mark Twain)

How true are these words.

Our work of correctly naming our projects and calling out their destiny is profound. Naming is a self-fulfilling prophecy.

PRECEPT SEVEN - GOD MADE

"God made the vault and separated the water under the vault from the water above it. And it was so" (Genesis 1:7). We are God made.

We are not self-made.

We are not *self*-made; we are men and women *God* made. When you make something, that thing has your personality in it. Similarly, every creature, tree, shrub, and animal has a touch of God's personality. But every human has something more—*the very essence* of God's nature and his likeness.

Whatever you make has your personality. That means it has your stamp of approval. You must be proud of it. God is very proud of you because he made you. You're his handiwork. God made you with grace and faith and not stress and strife. You are *a masterpiece* of God's creative genius; you were made for good works, and your path was laid out for you. This incredible verse proves it: "For we are God's handiwork, created in Christ Jesus to do good works, which God prepared in advance for us to do" (Ephesians 2:10).

Surely it must inspire and encourage you to know that you do not have to work things out; instead, things work out for you. You were not made to work for God but instead for God to work through you. This is how mighty things are accomplished. Your work, then, is allowing God to make something great out of you. Yes, it will cost you everything, but the rewards are endless. Letting God work through you is not only giving your heart to Jesus; it is also submitting your soul to him—giving him your intellect, your desires, and your will. It's saying "Lord, let not my will but your will be done." In other words, it's laying yourself at the altar as a living sacrifice and saying to him "Today I stop living and working *for you* and declare that my life will be about you living and working through me. Lord, I will stop fighting you as I am made by you."

Be humble before God.

I am not talking about you giving everything up and moving to a foreign country as a missionary. (Of course, if that is what God is telling you to do, then do it.) I am talking about humility—when one rids oneself of selfish ambition and pride.

Pride is a powerfully negative force that stops the goodness and greatness of God flowing to and through you. You make yourself humble before God and he makes you great before humankind. This is a mystery, but it is the only way to true victory. I often joke that we should just get out of God's way so that he can bless us.

When God Wants a Man

When God wants to drill a man,
And thrill a man,
And skill a man
When God wants to mold a man
To play the noblest part;
When He yearns with all His heart
To create so great and bold a man
That all the world shall be amazed,
Watch His methods, watch His ways!
How He ruthlessly perfects
Whom He royally elects!
How He hammers him and hurts him,
And with mighty blows converts him
Into trial shapes of clay which
Only God understands;
While his tortured heart is crying
And he lifts beseeching hands!

How He bends but never breaks
When his good He undertakes;
How He uses whom He chooses,
And which every purpose fuses him;
By every act induces him
To try His splendor out-
God knows what He's about.

—Original by Angela Morgan; pronouns replaced by John Oswald Sanders

There are many titles in this world, but the title above all others is "God Made."

PRECEPT EIGHT – GOD POSITIONED

"God set them in the vault of the sky to give light on the earth" (Genesis 1:17).

- Be where *God* wants you to be,
- do what *God* wants you to do, and
- live how *God* wants you to live.

Your proximity is crucial.

Most of the time we miss important opportunities because we do not recognize the Lord's positioning of us. God orders the footsteps of his people. Therefore, our work is to be sensitive to his leading and prompting and to be exactly where he wants us to be, even if it's uncomfortable, scary, or does not make sense. Instead of asking, "Lord! Why do I have to go there or stay in this position," it is better to ask "Lord, what are you showing me and who am I supposed to meet?"

Jesus gave us his most powerful strategy on positioning ourselves for success when he said,

> "Whatever city or village you enter, ask who in it is worthy [who welcomes you and your message], and stay at his house until you leave [that city]. As you go into the house, give it your greeting [that is, 'Peace be to this house']. If [the family living in] the house is worthy [welcoming you and your message], give it your [blessing of] peace [that is, a blessing of well-being and prosperity, the favor of God]. But if it is not worthy, take back your *blessing of* peace." (Matthew 10:11–13 AMP)

In real estate the secret to success is location, location, location! In living a life of *unwork,* I would say that it's position, position, position! Your correct positioning brings complete peace, prosperity, favor, and well-being to everyone around you. When God positions you, he is setting you up and placing you in perfect alignment so that your life's purposes unfold for his glory.

As I reflect upon my life, I can easily recognize the moments when God positioned me in the right place at the right time for the right reasons. Positioning is like a link in a chain that connects you from person to person, moment to moment, and victory to victory.

A bicycle!

When I was about fourteen years old, my mother saw an old bicycle for sale. It cost twenty-five dollars but she only had fifteen. Still, she said, "There is a bicycle for sale. I want to buy it for you. Let's go and see it." We walked to the place and the owner said it was twenty-five dollars. And then a miracle happened, which I will never forget. My mother took her money out and said to the man. "Mister, I have only fifteen dollars," and she placed it in the man's hand. The man counted it and had a puzzled look on his face, saying, "You just gave me twenty-five dollars." My mother, who lived a life of prayer and who witnessed mighty miracles throughout her life, smiled. "Well, I guess I did!" I loved my bicycle and used it for several years. Then I sold it and bought a better one.

One day I sensed I was to ride my bicycle into what was then under Apartheid South Africa, called a "White village." On the road was a group of men. One called out to me and said, "Young man, please sell me your beautiful bicycle." He offered me $100, and to a poor young man like me, it was as if he gave me a million dollars.

A few weeks later, I found myself outside a security training company offering programs for $100. I signed up. A month later, I turned eighteen and was out looking for a job. I hitched a ride into the big city. I walked more than four miles while knocking on company doors, but nobody would give me a job. Late that evening I sat on the roadside tired, hungry, and defeated. A vehicle stopped and I ran up to it. The man said to me, "Young fellow, what are you doing in this dangerous area?" I said that I was looking for a job in security.

He said, "Well, it so happens that I own a security company, but I do not know if I can employ you because you have no experience." For some reason he asked me my name, and when I told him, the man chuckled and said, "My name is Pillay as well. Now I have to give you a job." And he did.

I was positioned at a shopping mall working the night shift all by myself. It was horrible and extremely dangerous. But there was a restaurant at the back, and the manager really liked me. He fed me every night. He said to me, "Son, this is such a dangerous place. Why are you working here? I have a cousin who is a senior person at one of South Africa's largest security companies. Would you like me to ask him to arrange a good job for you?" I said yes. And he did.

The company was a large international company, and after my training, I was certified as a supervisor. But I was positioned very far from my home. Thankfully, I had an uncle who lived close by the company, and I was able to stay with him. Every day I walked past a hospital, and one day I recognized a man from my hometown who worked there. He got me a job at the hospital. I met a lady who ran a little food cart. She had a sister who lived close by and had a room for rent. I rented it. The owner of the house had a nephew living in New Zealand, and he introduced me to him. A few years later I went to New Zealand, found the Zig Ziglar tape, and became an international speaker. Today I advise highly successful business owners, public figures, and world leaders while travelling around the world teaching, speaking, and preaching the good news of Jesus Christ.

That, my friend, is the power of God positioning you. Every breakthrough and success I ever had came out of God positioning me exactly where he wanted me to be. *Our work is to be correctly positioned*.

PRECEPT NINE - GOD APPROVED

"And God saw that it was good" (Genesis 1:10). God blesses us because *he* is good, not because *we* did good. God looked at everything, approved it, and said it was good and very good. Our work is not to *do* good or *be* good, it is to *see ourselves* as good.

Over the years I have encountered tens of thousands of people, and the majority had one common stumbling block—they never felt they were good enough. Yes, even those who appeared confident and successful and in high positions—deep inside they felt the same no matter how much they did or gave or served. The majority of people live a life seeking the approval of others and, sadly, the criticism of others destroys them. Seeking other people's approval is hard work, and we will never be enough to them.

Be diligent–free of shame.

The apostle Paul said to young Timothy, "Be diligent to present yourself approved to God as a worker who does not need to be ashamed, accurately handling the word of truth" (2 Timothy 2:15 NASB). When we look at such a verse with religious-colored glasses, we instantly assume that we must do good works to please God and then he will approve of us. However, this is not the case. In the context of God's relationship with his children, being diligent does not mean working hard. It means to be eager or to be the first to say to yourself:

- ✓ I am good enough and have been approved by God.
- ✓ He has placed upon me his seal of approval, and I am worthy of my royal calling.
- ✓ I will not be ashamed of my past, or failures, or shortcomings.
- ✓ I will not be ashamed of Jesus and the truth of his gospel.

I once had lunch with an associate pastor of a megachurch. Halfway through our meal, I sensed a prompting in my spirit. With the words, *Tell him he is a good man*, I said, "Pastor, I sense the Lord lay on my heart to tell you that you are a good man." He stopped eating and nervously said, "Well, I do not think my wife would agree." Then a few minutes later, the same prompting came again. *Tell him that he is a good man*. Again I said to him, "Pastor, I sense the Lord lay on my heart to tell you that you are a good man." He stopped eating and said again, "I don't think my wife would agree."

We continued eating, and then, for the third time, I sensed the same prompting: *Tell him he is a good man*. I said "Pastor, the Lord laid on my heart these words: You are a good man." This time I noticed a change. Tears welled in his eyes, and he looked at me and said "Melvin, I am a good man." The moment he said these words, something lifted off him. He poured his heart out to me and confessed his fears, failures, and struggles. He said he'd never felt good enough for ministry because he was held prisoner of his past. He said when God saved him, he started working for God and wanted to be the best servant ever. As a result, he strived to be good so that he could please God, but whenever he made a mistake or sinned, he would live in total guilt and condemnation, feeling that God had rejected him and that he had to beg God for forgiveness.

By the grace of God, this precious pastor had a life-transforming moment at the table and was set free from the spirit of religion and the incorrect interpretation of God's Word. The Holy Spirit *convicts* us of our sins, and we must repent, but he never *condemns* us of our sins, and he will not put us through guilt trips.

Many are like this pastor—caught up in the struggle of just being a servant of God—while those who are free from this bondage sit at the table enjoying the feast prepared by God. Being a servant of God is the greatest honor. Being a child of God is the greatest privilege. Being a friend of God is the greatest mystery. Jesus no longer calls us servants, and he explained why:

> Jesus replied ... "I no longer call you servants, because a servant does not know his master's business. Instead, I have called you friends, for everything that I learned from my Father I have made known to you." (John 15:15)

Why would you want to live and work as a servant when you have been approved as a friend of God? Your work is not to work as a servant striving for approval. Your work is to be a friend approved by God.

PRECEPT TEN – GOD BLESSED

God blessed them and said, "Be fruitful and increase in number and fill the water in the seas, and let the birds increase on the earth" (Genesis 1:22). We do not work *to be* blessed; we *are* blessed, therefore we work.

To be blessed means to increase in joy and peacefulness and experience the kingdom of God being released upon a person or God's creation. We see the three kingdom attributes of righteousness, peace, and joy in the first psalm of David.

> Blessed [overflowing with joy and peace] is the one
> who does not walk in step with the wicked
> or stand in the way that sinners take
> or sit in the company of mockers,
> but whose delight is in the law of the Lord,
> and who meditates on his law day and night.
> That person is like a tree planted by streams of water,
> which yields its fruit in season
> and whose leaf does not wither—
> whatever they do prospers.
> Not so the wicked!
> They are like chaff
> that the wind blows away.
> Therefore the wicked will not stand in the judgment,
> nor sinners in the assembly of the righteous.

For the LORD watches over the way of the righteous,
but the way of the wicked leads to destruction.

(Psalm 1:1–6)

The result of a blessed life is we will prosper in whatever we do. However, there are three conditions that we are follow:

- **Firstly,** be careful not to listen to ungodly, humanistic teaching and counsel because it is wickedness.
- **Secondly,** make sure to not follow in the ways of sinful people who will lead many astray.
- **Thirdly,** do not sit in the company of people who mock, slander, and gossip because such people will impact many lives with foolishness.

In other words, if we reject these three conditions, we will remove ourselves from the blessed life and imprison ourselves under a curse.

The first three blessings of God

To live a life of *unwork,* one must understand the first three blessings of God. God, in his great wisdom, blessed the great sea creatures with a threefold blessing:

> God said, "Let the water teem with living creatures, and let birds fly above the earth across the vault of the sky." So God created the great creatures of the sea and every living thing with which the water teems and that moves about in it, according to their kinds, and every winged bird according

> to its kind. And God saw that it was good. God blessed them and said, "Be fruitful and increase in number and fill the water in the seas, and let the birds increase on the earth." (Genesis 1:20–22)

Blessing One: Be Fruitful

Being fruitful means that the power to produce and to increase in number is within you. Your offspring from within you will become a reality. Filling the water in the seas is a global mandate to spread out and populate the world.

So powerful was the first blessing that during the time of Noah, the sea creatures were not killed.

Blessing Two: A Fivefold Blessing

To Adam and Eve, God gave a fivefold blessing:

> God blessed [Adam and Eve], [granting them certain authority] and said to them, "Be fruitful, multiply, and fill the earth, and subjugate it [putting it under your power]; and rule over (dominate) the fish of the sea, the birds of the air, and every living thing that moves upon the earth." So God said, "Behold, I have given you every plant yielding seed that is on the surface of the entire earth, and every tree which has fruit yielding seed; it shall be food for you; and to all the animals on the earth and to every bird of the air and to everything that moves on the ground—to everything in which

> there is the breath of life—I have given every green plant for food"; and it was so [because He commanded it]. God saw everything that He had made, and behold, it was very good, and He validated it completely. And there was evening, and there was morning, a sixth day. (Genesis 1:28–30 AMP)

1. **Be fruitful.** The power to produce is within.
2. **Multiply.** You have unlimited ability to increase *with no limitations.*
3. **Fill the earth.** You have a global mandate to populate the earth *with no limitations.*
4. **Subjugate.** You have God's authority over whatever is yours.
5. **Rulership.** You get to care for and lead what is yours to victory and enjoy continuous prosperity.

Blessing Three: Rest

The third blessing is fascinating as it was not for a bird, fish, animal, or human. God blessed time, hours, minutes, and seconds. He called it the seventh day, the Sabbath.

The first time we see the word "work" in the Bible is when God rested from it. He separated time from the seven-day cycle and did not bless the six days of work. He blessed *the day of rest.* He also made it holy, and his very presence filled this space of time.

> By the seventh day, God had finished the work he had been doing; so on the seventh day he rested from all his work. Then God blessed the seventh day and made it holy because

> on it he rested from all the work of creating that he had done. (Genesis 2:2–3)

The animals were not blessed. The land was not blessed. Sea creatures and birds were blessed. Humans were blessed. Rest was blessed. Rest is the *finished* work of God.

8

THE SEVENFOLD BLESSING OF REST

Work is action. Rest is the finished work of God, and rest is blessed.

A few years ago I spoke at an event in San Diego. Afterwards, a lady came up to me and said "Melvin, I really enjoyed your talk about rest and the true meaning of work, but doesn't the Bible admonish us about work and say not to rest? And she quoted Proverbs 6:10–11:

> A little sleep, a little slumber,
> a little folding of the hands to rest—
> and poverty will come on you like a thief
> and scarcity like an armed man.

I replied, "What does Proverbs 6:9 say?" She looked confused, so we looked it up together, and she was relieved to know that King Solomon was admonishing the sluggards, the ones who were habitually lazy, and not those who were like her.

> How long will you lie there, you sluggard?
> When will you get up from your sleep?

> A little sleep, a little slumber,
> a little folding of the hands to rest—
> and poverty will come on you like a thief
> and scarcity like an armed man. (Proverbs 6: 9–11)

Rest Is the Very Presence of God

Rest is one of the most misunderstood things on earth. It is a place *in* God and a space made *by* God. He says that the wicked will never enter this place of rest and they will not enjoy the blessings of it. He reserves a place and a space for those whom he loves. Rest is the very presence of God.

When I started in the business world as a salesperson, I worked very hard—seven days a week and sixteen to eighteen hours a day. During the hours that I was not working, I read books on sales and success. I slept between two to three hours only. My friends would say, "Melvin, why don't you rest?" and I would foolishly say, "I will rest when I am dead." And then God got a hold of me and showed me a better way to live.

As I studied God's Word, I came across powerful scriptures that transformed me. Every time I picked up my Bible, I would find insightful verses on rest, such as these ones:

> Whoever dwells in the shelter of the Most High will rest in the shadow of the Almighty. (Psalm 91:1)

I thought to myself, *God is inviting me into his shelter and under his shadow—a place and space of rest he's given to me.*

And,

> Jesus said ... "Come to me, all you who are weary and burdened, and I will give you rest. Take my yoke upon you and learn from me, for I am gentle and humble in heart, and you will find rest for your souls. For my yoke is easy and my burden is light." (Matthew 11:28–30)

I realized that Jesus was offering me a most wise and winning strategy—*the path of least resistance*. He was saying that if I came to him, he would not give me hard work or strife or stress. Instead, he would give me rest. And he promised that his yoke of teaching would be easy and his burden of calling or work would be light. I'd never seen this before. I'd never thought that life and work, especially God's work, were easy and light and blessed with his rest.

I was always taught that God's work was the path of *most* resistance—a burden, hard, filled with pain and difficulties. I was taught that the devil would attack me every step of the way and that people would not like me and constantly be against me. But instead, Jesus was saying that I must work from his place of rest.

I believed every word that the Lord said and was very moved by this revelation. I said, "Lord, your Word says that you are my shepherd, and you will take care of all my needs and wants. I want to take a complete year off to study your Word and pray." I sensed him say, "Go ahead and do it." So, I stayed home and studied the Bible and prayed from 7 a.m. to 4 p.m. for an entire year. A few months into it, my friends said, "Melvin, why aren't you working?" and I told them that God would take care of me. They thought I was crazy.

But God *did* take care of me. My mortgage and car payments were always paid on time. I ate well and every need was met. In fact, I had money left over at the end of every month, which had not always happened when I worked. (It is important to note that God allowed me to take a year off to study and pray, and I am not suggesting that you do the same. He was preparing me for my life's purpose).

Kingdom Business

After my year of study, prayer, and immersion into a life of rest and of work being easy and light, I launched my kingdom business as a public speaker, coach, and sales trainer. I said to my friends, "God worked six days and rested one. I feel he is telling me to work one day and rest six days." They laughed, but little did I know that I was prophesying my destiny into reality. Today, decades later, I have worked no more than fifty-two days a year, and the returns are astronomical. My wife and I travel together throughout the world, living a life that's easy and light and blessed by rest.

Rest Is Blessed

When God blessed the seventh day with rest and made it holy, he made it the most important day of all days and set a pattern for us to observe and follow.

The day of rest is the most powerful day of the week. It gives us all the blessings that are needed to face the world during the week ahead. Experts from many fields have expressed their findings that a day of rest away from our work increases our creativity and problem-solving abilities. And a day away from electronic screens such as computers and smartphones is helpful in improving our focus.

The Sabbath day of rest is God's gift to us, and Jesus is the Lord over the day of rest. It is not a religious ritual that must be observed with drudgery and despair. It is a blessing, a day overflowing with joy and peace, a day of celebration and a time for family and friends and feasting. The day of Sabbath is the most important *unwork* day of the week. And those who make it a priority will live in the sevenfold blessing of their original design—before the fall of man.

It starts with the presence of God upon one's life. As we see in the life of Moses, "The LORD replied, 'My Presence will go with you, and I will give you rest'" (Exodus 33:14). When his presence is with us, the blessings overflow upon our lives, and we will experience the kingdom in our lives.

The Sevenfold Blessing

This is the sevenfold blessing that will unfold over you. It is the perfect alignment of God and you.

God's presence leads to
God's rest which leads to
God's peace which leads to
God's power which leads to
God's authority which leads to
God's prosperity which leads to
God's rulership.

The busyness of life keeps us away from the presence of God and we are thrown off alignment. Just like a vehicle that needs wheel alignment, all we must do is take our vehicle in for an alignment. So, too, all we must do is come into the presence of God to be perfectly aligned with him.

9

THE MAN OF UNWORK

Rest, ease, and light are only attained when our state of mind is at peace and not at war.

God's original design was for the ten precepts of work to come together and form:

- the powerful dynamic called *action* and
- the powerful *blessing* of being overshowed by the presence of God,

and to increase in joy and peacefulness. Work is action and *rest is blessed*.

Out of God's rest, humankind worshiped God through work *and rest*. God's presence set in motion:

- action,
- rest,
- fruitfulness,
- multiplication, and
- increase.

Out of Alignment

Sadly, after the fall of humankind, the first thing that was lost was the blessing of God's presence. "The LORD God called to [Adam], 'Where are you?'" (Genesis 3:9). For the first time in human history, humankind was no longer in the presence of their Creator.

Adam and Eve no longer lived in the presence of God; no longer did they have perfect alignment with God. And they lost the sevenfold blessing of,

God's presence, which led to
God's rest, which led to
God's peace, which led to
God's power, which led to
God's authority, which led to
God's prosperity, which led to
God's rulership.

They now lived in a new reality—the sevenfold curse, in which they were,

Void of God's presence, which led to
restlessness, which led to
conflict, which led to
weakness, which led to
demotion, which led to
poverty, which led to
subservience.

Here we see all the curses God spoke upon the serpent, the woman and the man, and the ground:

> The LORD God said to the serpent, "Because you have done this,
>
> "Cursed are you above all livestock
> and all wild animals!
> You will crawl on your belly
> and you will eat dust
> all the days of your life.
> And I will put enmity
> between you and the woman,
> and between your offspring and hers;
> he will crush your head,
> and you will strike his heel." (Genesis 3: 4–15)
>
> To the woman he said,
>
> "I will make your pains in childbearing very severe;
> with painful labor you will give birth to children.
> Your desire will be for your husband,
> and he will rule over you." (v. 16)
>
> To Adam he said, "Because you listened to your wife and ate fruit from the tree about which I commanded you, 'You must not eat from it,'
>
> "Cursed is the ground because of you;
> through painful toil you will eat food from it
> all the days of your life.

> It will produce thorns and thistles for you,
> and you will eat the plants of the field.
> By the sweat of your brow
> you will eat your food
> until you return to the ground,
> since from it you were taken;
> for dust you are
> and to dust you will return." (vv.17–19)

Friend, from all the things we could lose in this life—loved ones, health, money, relationships, time, and more; *the most painful of all is losing the presence of God.* This is why King David cried out,

> Create in me a clean heart, O God,
> And renew a right *and* steadfast spirit within me.
> Do not cast me away from Your presence
> And do not take Your Holy Spirit from me.
> Restore to me the joy of Your salvation
> And sustain me with a willing spirit. (Psalm
> 51:10–12 AMP)

Live Only in the Presence

No matter where you live, how you live, or how short you live, live daily in the presence of the Almighty.

The explorer and missionary David Livingstone spent thirty-three years in Africa. On May 1, 1873—in Chief Chitambo's village at Chipundu, southeast of Lake Bangweulu, Zambia—Livingstone preached a sermon and then went into his hut. Hours later people came to the evening service, but he was not there. They went to his hut looking for him. His people told the crowd not to disturb him because it was his custom to pray. Some time went by, and his servants were a bit concerned. They went into his room and saw him kneeling at his bedside. Nervously going up to him, one of them called out but then touched his shoulder and discovered that he was dead. And somebody captioned his life with these immortal words. "He died the way he lived, in the presence of his God."

The Curse Lifted

The goodness and mercy of God was displayed about 1,656 years after the fall of man and the curse of hard work. God rose a relatively unknown man by the name of Lamech, who did a very significant thing: he prophesied over the life and destiny of his son Noah.

> When Lamech was a hundred and eighty-two years old, he became the father of a son. He named him Noah, saying, "This one shall bring us rest and comfort from our work and from the [dreadful] toil of our hands because of the ground which the Lord cursed." (Genesis 5:28–29 AMP)

Through the grace of God, Lamech's prophesy changed the course of the entire world. The curse of hard work was broken as God moved upon the life of Noah.

We see the life of this powerful man of God:

> But Noah found favor in the eyes of the LORD. These are *the records of* the generations (family history) of Noah. Noah

> was a righteous man [one who was just and had right standing with God], blameless in his [evil] generation; Noah walked (lived) [in habitual fellowship] with God. Now Noah became the father of three sons: Shem, Ham, and Japheth. (Genesis 6:8–10 AMP)

Lamech's words brought favor upon Noah, and Noah lived righteously, blamelessly, and faithfully.

A Parent's Blessing

As I mentioned earlier, I believe that after the blessings of God the Father, the next most powerful blessing on earth is the blessings of one's parents. Parents have spiritual authority to speak the destiny of God into their children's lives.

After several years of living abroad, I went back to my home in South Africa to visit my parents. My mother was extremely ill and on her deathbed. She called me to her side and whispered a blessing, saying, "You must preach his gospel and do his will; that's why he made you." Those were her last words to me, and I did not share them with anyone. I went back to New Zealand, and a few days later my mother went home to be with Jesus. But her words burned in my heart like a fire shut up in my bones.

A few years later I went back to South Africa to visit my father. Just before I left him, he looked at me and said, "When I die, do not bother to come see a dead body. You must preach his gospel; that's why he made you." I never saw my father again because a year later, I started my ministry and was preaching my first sermon at a church

I'd started. It so happened that on that very Sunday—as I preached in Auckland, New Zealand—my father was being buried in South Africa. As I preached, I could still hear his words to me.

Today, decades later, that fire stills burns in my heart. By the grace of God, I have preached his gospel around the world to thousands of people because that's why he made me.

And God Blessed

- God spoke through Lamech to empower the life of Noah.
- God rose Noah to undo the curse of hard work.
- God blessed Noah and made a covenant with him and his sons and all living creatures.

The blessing included the return of God's presence, an increase of joy and peacefulness, and a restoration of fruitfulness, multiplication, increase, and rulership.

> God blessed Noah and his sons and said to them, "Be fruitful and multiply, and fill the earth. The fear and the terror of you shall be [instinctive] in every animal of the land and in every bird of the air; and together with everything that moves on the ground, and with all the fish of the sea; they are given into your hand. Every moving thing that lives shall be food for you; I give you everything, as I gave you the green plants and vegetables. (Genesis 9:1–3 AMP)

However, only much later was the curse completely broken, and humankind was redeemed by the crucifixion and resurrection of the Lord Jesus Christ.

10

FACING PHARAOH

We might think that as Christians, we are finally free from this curse of hard work, but we are not.

Something took the curse from the ground and placed it upon a man, who then placed it upon the world, and it's one of the most powerful spiritual forces in the world today—the spirit of Pharoah aka mammon.

A Most Interesting Dream

In early 2020, I dreamed that I was asleep, in a room with several other people. I saw a fifteen-foot brown cobra making its way among all the people, but everyone was soundly sleepy, so nobody could see this cobra. I began yelling at the people saying, "Get up! Get up! There is a venomous cobra here about to kill you." The cobra slithered over the people but did not bite them. A few people got up and laughed at me, thinking that I was only joking. A few people saw the cobra and a spirit of apathy covered over them and they said, "Nothing will happen to us," and went back to their slumber.

I yelled even louder, but nobody seemed to care, and all went back to sleep. I was tired and went back to sleep myself (still in my dream). I felt something on my head, and I looked around and saw the cobra was now trying to swallow me. It was going after my head. I got up and shook it off, and it fell to the ground. I felt the atmosphere in the room change and sensed the spirit of God enter it, leading me to feel overwhelming love and peace and joy. The Spirit went up to the cobra and asked it, "What are you doing here?" And the cobra shrank from a massive serpent into a tiny, two-inch long worm. Then the Spirit turned to me and said only one word, "Genesis." And the dream ended.

The following morning, I got up and wrote down the dream and pondered and then opened the book of Genesis, reading on to the book of Exodus. As I read, two names stood out: Moses and Pharoah. And so did the words Moses said to Pharoah: "Then the Lord said to Moses, 'Go, tell Pharaoh king of Egypt to let the Israelites go out of his country'" (Exodus 6:10–11). As I prayed, God revealed that the spirit of Pharoah is the prince over America and the nations. I remembered the Book of Daniel and his mentioning the Prince of Persia, and how the angel fought with this prince for twenty-one days and got the victory.

I continued to study the book of Genesis over the next few days. Still drawn to the name Pharoah, I thought about my dream of the cobra, and God revealed that the cobra in my dream was the spirit of Pharaoh. I then researched the word "Pharoah" and discovered that it was a title given to the ruler of ancient Egypt and meant "his majesty," "his royalty," and "the lord of two lands." On the crown of Pharaoh was a brown cobra, which is associated with the sun god and is a symbol of protection. In addition, my research led me to a very interesting revelation—*Pharoah, the spirit of this age, was the descendant of Ham, the cursed son of Noah.*

The Sons of Noah

The three sons of Noah who came out of the ark were Shem, Ham, and Japheth. (Ham was the father of Canaan.) From them came the people who were scattered over the whole earth.

> Noah, a man of the soil, proceeded to plant a vineyard. When he drank some of its wine, he became drunk and lay uncovered inside his tent. Ham, the father of Canaan, saw his father naked and told his two brothers outside. But Shem and Japheth took a garment and laid it across their shoulders; then they walked in backward and covered their father's naked body. Their faces were turned the other way so that they would not see their father naked.
>
> When Noah awoke from his wine and found out what his youngest son had done to him, he said,
>
> "Cursed be Canaan!
> The lowest of slaves
> will he be to his brothers."
>
> He also said,
>
> "Praise be to the Lord, the God of Shem!
> May Canaan be the slave of Shem.
> May God extend Japheth's territory;

> may Japheth live in the tents of Shem,
> and may Canaan be the slave of Japheth."
> (Genesis 9:18–27)

Noah cursed his son Ham because of the evil that was done to him. And the curse of painful toil and hard work that God placed on the land was now placed on a man—Ham. Ham was to be yoked to the burden of hard work, and the sevenfold curse was now upon him and his descendants. He was:

> **Void of God's presence**, which led to
> **restlessness**, which led to
> **conflict**, which led to
> **weakness**, which led to
> **demotion**, which led to
> **poverty**, which led to
> **subservience**.

Ham, the cursed son, become the father of the Hamites, who were the Canaanites, who became the children of Egypt; and out of this was born the title "Pharoah," aka Mammon Ra, the slave driver, the god of this world worshipped by governments, corporations, and the multitudes. Today the spirit of Pharaoh-Mammon-Ra—is alive and well. But we can be set free and live a life that is blessed with rest and *unwork*.

The Force That Breaks the Yoke

Unwork is the revelation and the force which breaks the yoke of Pharoah-Mammon-Ra.

We must face Pharoah, take the victory Jesus won for us, and live in freedom.

It is time we recognized what mammon has done to us and how we are bound to this spirit. We live controlled by bills and are afraid of trusting God and stepping out in faith to do his will. We have been too conditioned to work for money to pay our bills instead of trusting God to care for our needs and wants.

It is time that we stopped wondering where the money will come from and instead start worshipping God and thanking him for his goodness and mercy. He gives wealth to those who trust in him alone. It is time that we started believing what God says in his Word and got rid of doubt, fear, unbelief, and faithlessness.

God is more real than any reality.

God is more powerful than any other power.

God is able to do more than you can imagine and envision.

Only believe.

Hard work is an obsession and an addiction for so many people, and even though we try to overcome it, we often fail because guilt sets in and condemnation tells us that it's our responsibility, and that if something goes wrong, it's all our fault. Some people have worked so hard for so long, and so diligently, they cannot even recognize this curse upon their lives because it feels so normal and right. It feels as if we are doing it for others, so how can it be a bad thing? But it is a curse.

It has conditioned us, and bad habits have been formed within us.

Friend, no one can serve two masters. We have to make a decision to follow God the Father or "the god mammon." "No one can serve two masters; for either he will hate the one and love the other, or else he will be loyal to the one and despise the other. You cannot serve God and mammon" (Matthew 6:24 AMP). It is foolish of us to gain the world and lose the kingdom.

Give your mind, body, emotions, spirit, time, and will to God. God will renew your mind and you will be set free.

Freedom from Pharoah-Mammon-Ra

I have recognized that,

how we think determines
how we feel, which determines
how we speak, which determines
how we practice, which becomes
our habits and determines
our success and failures.

We can be free from the slave master Pharoah-Mammon-Ra by changing the way we think. We usually see ourselves as CEO slaves, employee slaves, self-employed slaves, and ministry slaves. When we fix our mind and clear the trash that's in our head, we are setting ourselves up for freedom. We can echo the words Moses said to Pharoah. "The Lord said to Moses, 'Go to Pharaoh and say to him, "This is what the Lord, the God of the Hebrews, says: 'Let my people go, so that they may worship me'"'" (Exodus 9:1).

Neurologists tell us that what we do in the first thirty minutes of waking up in the morning will have a lasting impact on the rest of our day and create long-lasting habits. As I mentioned before, impactful thoughts can be formed in as few as seven minutes. The good news is that all it takes is just seven minutes a day over a seven-day period to make significant changes in your thought life and fix the mind.

11

FREEDOM SEVEN

Capture your thoughts.

Free Your Mind

This simple yet effective daily exercise will help change your life and bring freedom. It will help you to think-feel-speak-practice-perform-succeed God's way in a very short period of time. The secret is to capture your "first" thoughts the moment you wake up. These thoughts are powerful because they dominate your day. They are very often mediocre or negative or fleeting. Replace these thoughts with kingdom power thoughts—God's thoughts.

Do the exercise that starts on the next page for the next seven days. The moment you wake up, turn to this chapter and the day you are on.

Day 1: Kingdom Power Thought 1

> "To the person who pleases him, God gives wisdom, knowledge and happiness; but to the sinner he gives the task of gathering and storing up wealth to hand it over to the one who pleases God. This too is meaningless, a chasing after the wind" (Ecclesiastes 2:26).

1. Read this Kingdom Power verse.
2. Think deeply about this verse for a minimum of seven minutes.
3. Capture the positive thoughts and feelings.
4. Write down the positive thoughts and feelings.

5. Speak out the positive thoughts and feelings.

Kingdom Power Thought 2

"Jesus answered, 'The work of God is this: to believe in the one he has sent'" (John 6:29).

1. Read this Kingdom Power verse.
2. Think deeply about this verse for a minimum of seven minutes.
3. Capture the positive thoughts and feelings.
4. Write down the positive thoughts and feelings.

5. Speak out the positive thoughts and feelings.

Kingdom Power Thought 3

"I sent you to reap what you have not worked for. Others have done the hard work, and you have reaped the benefits of their labor" (John 4:38).

1. Read this Kingdom Power verse.
2. Think deeply about this verse for a minimum of seven minutes.
3. Capture the positive thoughts and feelings.
4. Write down the positive thoughts and feelings.

5. Speak out the positive thoughts and feelings.

Kingdom Power Thought 4

"It is the LORD's blessing that makes a person rich, and hard work adds nothing to it" (Proverbs 10:22 GWT).

1. Read this Kingdom Power verse.
2. Think deeply about this verse for a minimum of seven minutes.
3. Capture the positive thoughts and feelings.
4. Write down the positive thoughts and feelings.

5. Speak out the positive thoughts and feelings.

Kingdom Power Thought 5

"I no longer call you servants, because a servant does not know his master's business. Instead, I have called you friends, for everything that I learned from my Father I have made known to you" (John 15:15).

1. Read this Kingdom Power verse.
2. Think deeply about this verse for a minimum of seven minutes.
3. Capture the positive thoughts and feelings.
4. Write down the positive thoughts and feelings.

5. Speak out the positive thoughts and feelings.

Kingdom Power Thought 6

"That person is like a tree planted by streams of water, which yields its fruit in season and whose leaf does not wither— whatever they do prospers" (Psalm 1:3).

1. Read this Kingdom Power verse.
2. Think deeply about this verse for a minimum of seven minutes.
3. Capture the positive thoughts and feelings.
4. Write down the positive thoughts and feelings.

5. Speak out the positive thoughts and feelings.

Kingdom Power Thought 7

"We are His workmanship [His own master work, a work of art], created in Christ Jesus [reborn from above—spiritually transformed, renewed, ready to be used] for good works, which God prepared [for us] beforehand [taking paths which He set], so that we would walk in them [living the good life which He prearranged and made ready for us]" (Ephesians 2:10 AMP).

1. Read this Kingdom Power verse.
2. Think deeply about this verse for a minimum of seven minutes.
3. Capture the positive thoughts and feelings.
4. Write down the positive thoughts and feelings.

5. Speak out the positive thoughts and feelings.

6. The Word of God will become alive, and hard work will become weaker in you and will eventually be nonexistent. Soon you will be what God made you to be, living a life of *unwork* and enjoying the sevenfold blessing of rest.

 God's presence leads to **God's rest,** which leads to **God's peace,** which leads to **God's power,**
 which leads to **God's authority**, which leads to
 God's prosperity, which leads to **God's rulership.**

There you go, my friend. This is the meaning of *unwork*.

- Remember! Hard work is a curse.
- Remember! Work is action.
- Remember! Rest is blessed.

Friend, our work is to wait for the Lord and be intertwined with him. This means that it is God working through you and the world sees God in all your work. When God does all the work, God gets all the glory.

When you work God's way and rest God's way, you will achieve momentum—a powerful dynamic. Momentum is set in motion by the hand of God. The sun, moon, ocean waves, and ever-flowing rivers all move effortlessly and successfully day after day, year after year. Likewise, the person with momentum is set on the path of least resistance. *Unwork* gives you momentum.

12

UNWORK TODAY

Think right, pray right, work right, and live right. Unwork is more than right; it's righteous.

My friend, as we come to the end of our time together, remember that your state of mind is the key to living a life of *unwork*. And it takes wisdom, willingness, and willpower to make a permanent change, but through the power of God within you, you can change and live in freedom. These five insights will help your state of mind be focused and perfectly aligned to the freedom and joy of *unwork*. Read them often.

#1 Be a Friend

"Then the LORD said: 'I am making a covenant with you. Before all your people, I will do wonders never before done in any nation in all the world. The people you live among will see how awesome is the *work* that I, the LORD, will do for you'" (Exodus 34:10, emphasis added). No longer are we slaves or only servants of God; we are his covenant friends.

All that is yours is God's; all that is God's is yours. Think about this always! Stop working *for* God and start walking *with* God.

#2 GRACE over Hard Work

"God treated me with undeserved grace! He made me what I am, and his grace wasn't wasted. I worked much harder than any of the other apostles, although it was really God's grace at work and not me" (1 Corinthians 15:10 CEV). It's not our outstanding work ethic or hard work that makes us great. It is God's grace at work in us. God's grace is enough. Hard work is never enough!

#3 Stop Being a Slave to Work

You cannot do God's work. He does his work through you. "He who worked effectively for Peter and empowered him in his ministry to the Jews also worked effectively for me and empowered me in my ministry to the Gentiles)" (Galatians 2:8 AMP).

God is at work in you, through you, and for you! Why does he do this? It's not complicated; it's because he loves you and it glorifies the name of Jesus.

#4 Prioritize Sleep

> Unless the Lord builds the house,
> They labor in vain who build it;
> Unless the Lord guards the city,
> The watchman keeps awake in vain.
>
> It is vain for you to rise early,
> To retire late,

> To eat the bread of anxious labors—
> For He gives [blessings] to His beloved *even in his* sleep.
> (Psalm 127:1–2 AMP)

The human will is powerful. We can think and work ourselves into great success, but if the Lord does not build it, it is all in vain. Every moment of our painful toil is an absolute waste of time and life. Sleep is a wonderful thing; it is a blessing from the Lord. Do not fight it. Enjoy it.

#5 Give up Independence

> From days of old no one has heard, nor has ear perceived,
> Nor has the eye seen a God besides You,
> Who works *and* acts in behalf of the one who [gladly] waits for Him. (Isaiah 64:4 AMP)

Our work is to gladly wait *in* the Lord. As I said earlier to *Wait in* means to intertwine with God, like two ropes wrapped together with no end and no beginning—perfect unity.

God's work is to release his angels to work and act for you. "Are not all angels ministering spirits sent to serve those who will inherit salvation?" (Hebrews 1:4). Work is hard when you do the work that only angels were created to do. May the Lord remove the spirit of independence and impulsiveness and grace you with patience and peace.

Gladly *wait* "in" the Lord. When you learn how to rest in God, he will teach you how he works for *you*.

BONUS CHAPTER

THE FIVE UNWORK LAWS FOR BUSY LEADERS

As an individual, you can incorporate all the *unwork* insights and wisdom into your daily life, but if you lead an organization, then these five laws are a must for you to follow:

1. Collaborate.
2. Network globally.
3. Build winning relationships.
4. Build up teams.
5. Do not manage.

#1 Collaborate

There's no greater feeling than being your own boss, but there is one big issue—the majority of leaders find themselves isolated and even alone. Leaders have defied the odds and pioneered for so long, but it is vital for such people to join other likeminded kingdom business leaders and unwork together. Partnering with other true kingdom leaders is powerful and gives a person much more leverage and freedom.

#2 Network Globally

We have heard that the world is our oyster. It is one of the most powerful strategies to cultivate vast numbers of different networks. Get involved in strategic networks. Success is not just what you know; it's also who you know and, more importantly, who they know. Great networkers have a pool of talent and robust networks that they draw on when a need arises.

#3 Build Winning Relationships

Success is 80 percent likability. When people like you, they will trust you; when they trust you, they will listen to you. When they listen to you, they will follow you and support you. Be likable and spend your life building other people up. Invest time, money, and resources in people. As Zig Ziglar often said, "You can have everything in life you want if you will just help enough other people get what they want."

#4 Team Building

You cannot do it on your own. Great leaders know that not everybody on the team is the same. Therefore, they have three categories of people. As an example, Jesus had different categories of friends, and so did King David.

- Jesus had a close group of three which included Peter, John, and Andrew; then the remaining nine disciples', followed by seventy more.King David had a close group of three—Yoshev-Bashevet,

El'azar, and Shammah—then twenty-seven, followed by a total leadership team of thirty-seven.

I call these categories: The Inner Circle, The Outer Circle, and the Outer Court.

a) **The Inner Circle**

These are three of your most loyal and faithful people, the hand-picked ones that you like the most and they like you the most. They trust you and you trust them. They love and respect you and very seldom challenge you when you are wrong. They will stay with you through it all and will almost never leave you. These are the big picture people, the momentum builders, the action takers who are ready to run and conquer and plunder for you.

b) **The Outer Circle**

These are the ones who are the "detail" people. They execute the plan and make sure everything runs smoothly. Unlike your inner circle, these people are not that into you. They respect and admire you, but they are focused on the objectives, goals, and tasks, and on completing the mission. They will challenge you and point out your flaws and errors. They have a strong sense of responsibility to the entire team and clients. They are advocates for others, asking questions like "Are we a socially responsible team" or "How can we be a better team for our clients." They are invaluable because they are the counterbalance and will ensure compliance and help weed out all the wrongs that may be in your life and business.

c) **The Outer Courts**

These are the doers. They are not interested in office politics; they're just here to work and earn money. They enjoy working with you but always have an eye open for another opportunity elsewhere. They are not fully committed to you or loyal to the team. They are drifters and will always move on.

It's crucial to know which group people belong to. If you position a person in the wrong group, you will have more problems than you would like to have.

#5 Do Not Manage

Nobody likes to be managed. What people are looking for is someone who can lead. Most leaders will not admit it, but they are control freaks. Learning how to stop micromanaging is a challenge, and it's why so many leaders are stressed due to worry, anxiety, and fear. The result is that a leader is juggling several different projects at a time, and with so many irons in the fire, they are less effective. They live under the power of mammon and hard work instead of a life of *unwork*. I advise leaders to use this simple strategy to rid themselves of the craziness: Write down all your projects, even ones from years gone by, then follow this plan:

- **Delegate** – Some projects are urgent and time sensitive. Select the right person ASAP and hand over control of the project to them. Don't undermine the person in charge or overwhelm them with constant requests and changes or demands. Trust them to deliver.

- **Relegate** – There are projects which may be important but not urgent. These must be correctly prioritized and set aside to lower priority.
- **Eliminate** – It's important to say goodbye to some projects or clients, no matter how close to your heart they may be. If it's eating up your time, money, resources, or peace, just get rid of it *now* and do not look back with any regrets. Just let go.
- **Update** – Set scheduled times to meet with your team to get updates and give insights. Nobody should be calling you out of these set times unless it's an emergency. It's also a good time to evaluate all your projects.
- **Automate** – We must use technology to simplify our lives. With today's rapid technological advancements, it is crucial that you not spend the time saved trying to learn about every new technology. Instead, find someone who can assist and do it for you.

EPILOGUE

DAILY OBSERVE THESE PRECEPTS AND INSIGHTS

The kingdom of God creates the path of least resistance.

The power to produce has been set in motion by God. He does not need our occupation; he needs our obedience.

- Be where God wants you to be.
- Do what God wants you to do.
- Live how God wants you to live.

Jesus said,

> "This is what the kingdom of God is like. A man scatters seed on the ground. Night and day, whether he sleeps or gets up, the seed sprouts and grows, though he does not know how. All by itself, the soil produces grain—first the stalk, then the head, then the full kernel in the head. As soon as the grain is ripe, he puts the sickle to it because the harvest has come." (Mark 4:26–29)

Enter this realm. Live in this reality. Walk in this rhythm. The kingdom is at work, so you can *unwork*.

Your friend,

Melvin Pillay—the most rested and *unworked* friend of God. *Selah*

ABOUT MELVIN PILLAY

Melvin is an East Indian, born in poverty during the deep years of Apartheid in South Africa. His mother, a recent convert to Christianity, kept her family fed during those lean times—not by scrounging for food or begging, but through prayer. She would wake her children up at 5 a.m., they would begin to pray, and by 8 a.m. food would show up, much like the legendary George Mueller's experience. Melvin had deep ambitions for success, which were only further fueled when his older brother, law student and economic hope of the entire family, tragically drowned.

Melvin moved to New Zealand and started in the world of sales. For a long time he was an abject failure. His boss secretly allowed him to sleep on the company floor, as long as he was dressed and ready for work before any of the other employees showed up.

A major turning point occurred when Melvin discovered a Zig Ziglar cassette tape in the Auckland library. He rented it with his last two dollars (instead of eating that day) and dug into it with fervor. As he listened to Zig—and as he began to sense the spiritual foundation behind Zig's message—he made a vow: Someday I will meet that man.

ONLY SEVEN YEARS LATER

Melvin found himself at a conference where the VP of Ziglar personally invited Melvin to be one of Ziglar's hand-selected trainers. Today Melvin is one of only eight such Platinum Zig Ziglar Speakers/Trainers.

Melvin ties together three powerful streams: His Eastern culture and lineage, which uniquely honed his spiritual perceptions; the wealth and knowledge of having worked with leaders from around the globe; and the Zig Ziglar business culture, which empowers him to cross many lines and move among many kinds of people.

Today Melvin not only does keynote speeches and trains and equips men and women to sell and to run their companies with fervor; he also mentors them in the ways of intuitive wisdom and brings unique, fire-branded methods that must be experienced to be understood. His one-on-one personal Whiteboard Session is a must for those who carry large loads in today's high-pressure, high-speed economy.

www.melvinpillay.com

MELVIN'S PROGRAMS

UNWORK WITH MELVIN

Are you ready to *unwork* with Melvin, unlearn the junk, un-grind from the rat race, understand yourself, and be free?

Melvin is available to do keynote talks, and has several Easy and Light consulting, coaching, and mastermind programs around the world.

THE WHITEBOARD WITH MELVIN PILLAY

The Whiteboard Session is an in-depth spiritual, mental, emotional, and practical optimization and equipping session designed to help move a person from promise to fulfillment and provide insights on establishing a lasting legacy for God's glory.

The Whiteboard Session is unique and tailored for the individual. No two people will have the same experience. The entire session is based on God's revelation and not on human wisdom or knowledge.

Over the past two decades, Melvin has worked with business leaders, entrepreneurs, and government leaders in a unique coaching format to help unlock the potential God has placed in their lives.

Over the course of the Whiteboard Session, you will:

- Cover your timeline—past, present, and future—and discover God's promises and purpose for your life.
- Identify and activate your current gifts.
- Find the conditions for your journey.
- Uncover the obstacles in your path.
- Layout a strategic and prophetic blueprint that will help lead you from promise to fulfillment.
- Help lay a foundation for your family legacy and future generations.

LIFE AFTER SUCCESS

Life after Success is an in-depth mental, spiritual, emotional, and practical optimization and equipping program designed to help high achievers, public figures, CEOs, and business owners transition from success to significance, and provide insights and guidance on establishing a lasting legacy.

Availability

Direct access to Melvin. You will get 1–2 personal text messages from Melvin per week with words of knowledge, words of encouragement, and insights.

Monthly Peer Group Call

Join a monthly, peer group power call with other seasoned, wealthy, and highly successful achievers for a time of encouragement, connection, and reflection.

Weekly Video Teaching

Get a weekly, short video teaching from Melvin focused on spiritual, mental, and emotional growth.

Personal Development

- Mind fixit
- Head recycle
- Mental wealth
- Finding true identity
- Finding purpose

Becoming Yoda

- Being a divine advisor
- Achieving excellent family culture
- Being a master communicator
- Being the meister
- Connecting your profession, life, and purpose

Back Office Support

A–Z admin, marketing, sales, and team working for you, so you can *unwork*.

GET ACTIVATED WITH MELVIN PILLAY

Join a global community of believers and kingdom-minded people who want to build their business God's way. We will work on some exciting topics like biblical wealth. You will get the kingdom precepts and the practices on how you can create dynamic systems so that you can produce wealth—not just for you or your grandchildren but also for generations to come.

Also, we will work on fascinating topics like "Easy and Light," and how you can build a kingdom business using the beautiful principles of Easy and Light—these amazing things God gives us to where we become exempt from the things other people have to face. You will also learn about spiritual warfare. You will tap into the dynamic power God has for you to build your business and leadership: tearing down the powers of the enemy, and silencing the inner voice and the inner demons of self-doubt, Wuhan fear, and unbelief. You will learn how you can build a kingdom business, and make it fireproof and bulletproof through any economy, by learning how God wants you to do his business. Additionally, you will be part of a strong community of people like you who understand you.

You will acquire insights of such topics like:

— How to build business (or do your work) God's way

— How to produce wealth for generations, not just for this week or month
— Precepts of "easy" and "light"
— How to do spiritual warfare and tear down strongholds
— How to overcome worry, fear, and belief

As a member of Melvin's Get Activated community, you will receive:

✓ **Community Platform**

Stay connected to your tribe on our online platform, where you can ask questions and get advice, insights, and prayer.

✓ **Monthly Group Web Conference Call**

Join a monthly group conference call with encouragement, teaching, and prayer.

✓ **Weekly Video Teaching**

Get a weekly short video teaching from Melvin focused on spiritual warfare, biblical wealth, and Easy and Light kingdom practices.

✓ **Additional Benefits Include:**

Discounted admission to our Get Activated conference and other events.

Please email us at support@melvinpillay.com or go to www.melvinpillay.com.

Printed in Great Britain
by Amazon

41697770R10086